My Faith
as an African

Jean-Marc Éla

*Translated from the French
by John Pairman Brown and Susan Perry*

ORBIS BOOKS

Maryknoll, New York 10545

GEOFFREY CHAPMAN

London SW1P 1RT UK

Originally published as *Ma foi d'Africain*. Copyright 1985 Éditions Karthala, 22-24 boulevard Arago, 75013 - Paris.

English translation copyright © 1988 by Orbis Books, Maryknoll, NY 10545

Published in the United States of America by Orbis Books, Maryknoll, New York 10545

Published in Great Britain in 1989 by Geoffrey Chapman, an imprint of Cassell Publishers Limited, Artillery House, Artillery Row, London SW1P 1RT.

Manuscript editor: Susan Perry

Library of Congress Cataloging-in-Publication Data

Éla, Jean-Marc, 1936–
  My faith as an African.

  Translation of: Ma foi d'Africain.
  Includes index.
  1. Christianity—Africa, Sub-Saharan. 2. Liberation
theology. I. Title.
BR1430.E4313 1988   276.7   88-31402

ORBIS/ISBN 0-88344-6316
CHAPMAN/ISBN 0 225 66566 2

Contents

Acknowledgments   **vii**

Foreword   **ix**
  by Simon E. Smith, S.J.

Preface   **xiii**

Part I
Reawakening the Wellsprings

1. An Itinerary   **3**
  The Progression of the Mission and the Challenge
    of the Poor   3
  The Sacrament of Community   6
  Notes   12

2. The Ancestors and Christian Faith   **13**
  African Symbolism   14
  Living in Christ Our Relationship with the Dead   18
  The Role of Sacrifice and the Diviner   21
  Christian Life and the Transformation of African
    Society   24
  An African Style of Celebration   26
  The Ancestors and the Veneration of the Saints   28
  A New Language for the Gospel   29
  Notes   31

3. Telling the Story of God's Revelation   **33**
  Black African Symbolism   34

Symbolism of the Physical World   37
Symbolism in the Initiation Ritual   40
Reawakening the Wellsprings of Existence   41
Toward a Living Relationship between Humanity
    and God   44
Toward an African Liturgy   47
A Faith for the Whole Person   50
Notes   52

4. The Future of Local Communities   **55**
Ending the Tyranny of the Clergy   55
Leadership within the Christian Community   60
Notes   64

Part II
Faith at the Grassroots

5. The Health of Those without Dignity   **67**
The Medical System and the Social System   67
Christian Missions and Health Programs   75
Sickness and Sin in the Bible   77
Underdevelopment: The Locus of God's Healing Will   80
A Challenge for the Churches: Mistrust Our Motives   83
Notes   85

6. The Granary Is Empty   **87**
"Africa Strangled": The Peasants   88
The Confrontation of Cultures and the Irruption
    of the Poor   90
A Ministry of the Granary   92
Popular Resistance and Creativity   97
The Cross of the Third World   99
Notes   101

7. Is God Neutral?   **102**
The Gospel at the Heart of the Conflict   105
Viewing the World from the Cross   108
Notes   112

Part III
Christianity Faces the Challenges of Africa

8. The Gospel Is at the Heart of Conflicts   **115**
The Basic Conflict between Rich and Poor   115
A Time for Change   120
A Break Is Needed   121
The Calvary of a People   123
Witnessing to the Lord of Life   126
Christianity Must Be Credible   130
Notes   135

9. The Generations of Independence   **137**
The African Church's Search for a Relevant Faith   138
Problems for the People—Questions Unanswered
    by Early Evangelization   140
Time for a Parting of the Ways   142
Where Do We Begin?   143
The Pitfalls of Africanization   145
Taking on the Challenges of Tomorrow's Generations   148
Can Christianity Be Based on the "Periphery"?   151
The Role of African Christian Youth   156
Notes   157

10. Speaking about God to Africans   **160**
Requirements of Our Faith as Africans   162
The Risk of an African Interpretation   165
Inculturation Set Adrift   170
A Theology Coming from the People   174
Notes   177

Conclusion: Theology under the Tree   **179**
Note   182

Index   **183**

Acknowledgments

The translators would like to acknowledge the unique contributions of Simon E. Smith, S.J. and Joseph Atanga, S.J. to the translation. Their understanding of the theological language and regional expressions used by the author was indispensable to the accuracy of the final text.

Foreword

Liberation theology is not exportable. Its very methodology demands that it commence from an analysis of the given concrete reality of a specific place or people or region.

When the Ecumenical Association of Third World Theologians (EATWOT) began in Dar es Salaam in 1976,[1] it was immediately clear that the Africans present were not all that comfortable with the terms used by Latin American liberation theologians. Some outsiders said that Africa "is not yet ready" for liberation theology—a statement as imperious as the imperialisms against which liberation theologians of Latin America, or anywhere else, struggle.

The problem at Dar, however, was more complex. Africa's poverty and oppression are both deeper and broader than we outsiders imagine. Engelbert Mveng, S.J., calls it "anthropological impoverishment": Africans have been robbed of their culture and thus even their human identity by a history of colonialism and exploitation which is not yet fully over.

Jean-Marc Éla is even more forceful in exposing this reality of excessive exploitation, both external and internal, in his *African Cry*[2] as well as in several other volumes.[3] He returns to the task in this collection of essays, lectures and addresses—one far more consistent and cohesive than most such ensembles. He approaches the task from a base of ten years of pastoral activity among the Kirdi of northern Cameroon where he was apprentice and then successor to "Baba Simon," a truly great modern indigenous apostle. And the result is a kind of liberation theology with an African face.

"Basic Christian Communities" are likewise a non-exportable phenomenon, even granted their apparent origin in Brazil and other Latin American countries. Yet they are growing in Africa. Both Bishop Patrick Kalilombe, M.Afr., and Fr. Joseph Healey,

M.M., have taken pains to spell out the uniqueness of their shape and progress in Africa. Éla brings us right into their midst, without bothering about labels ("basic" or "small" or whatever). The experience of walking with him on his journey is refreshing and enlightening.

His faith in God, the gospel, and especially the people themselves who suffer silently from hunger, marginalization, impoverishment, "modernization," alienation, up-rooting, flight, fear, etc., is both profound and eloquent. He speaks with clarity and conviction. He takes us by the hand into village Africa, helps us feel the painful reality behind the statistics of exploitation, and shares with us the pragmatic grounding of his conviction that every authentic inculturation of the Christian faith is conditioned on the liberation of the oppressed.

Thanks to EATWOT and its sister, the Ecumenical Association of African Theologians (whose *Bulletin of African Theology* is still not widely known in the English-speaking world), we of the north are only now discovering an Africa which reaches far beyond that of the anthropologists, sociologists, historians and missionary chroniclers. We are learning at last, through Éla and his brothers and sisters, of a new Africa, alive, indeed vibrant with faith. We are learning that inculturation is not just tinkering with liturgical externals, but reaches into the very depths of identity.

There is a strong affinity between American Black Theology and that of South Africa, still struggling for its liberation from *apartheid*. And there is a different, very distinct theology being articulated in the rest of sub-Saharan Africa, mostly by francophone theologians. Éla is at this time *facile princeps* of that wave. His peers are many, articulate, and sometimes aggressive[4]—but not yet well-known in our country. Thanks to *African Cry* and now *My Faith as an African*, we can really feel faith in the raw, uncompromising, totally committed, often indignant or angry, never despairing . . . and uniquely African.

As the preparations for an African Synod or Council, to be held in a couple of years, proceed apace, Éla's book will be indispensable for those who would understand what is at issue, for the agenda of both the Synod and Éla's words go far beyond the type of questions which stimulate *our* curiosity (dancing and drums at mass, polygamy, etc.) to touch directly at the heart of the matter: how to be and remain both Christian and African, how to recapture the uniqueness of African character amid forces which alienate, how to survive as humans amid economic and political structures which strangle, how to *be* who we are with joy and solidarity and fullness of life.

Half the world's 12,000,000 refugees are in Africa! Uprooted. Forced to flee. Strangers in their own continent. Bereft of land, family, friends, future. Éla's grappling with the forces which cause such de-humanization is instructive. Inspiring, indeed! For he faces head-on the entrapment of Africa's peoples in nets both made in Africa and imported from abroad. His *J'accuse* is telling, for he frankly criticizes the dehumanizing effects of the lust for power, the extravagant spending (both personal and state) of ruling élites, and their consequent negation of African familial and tribal solidarity. In other words, he exposes the underside of "progress" and contrasts it with gospel and African values. Hard reading. Sometimes sad. Always engrossing . . . and laying out a very demanding agenda for the future of Africa, if it is to survive as African.

We of the north are in his debt, for our media pay so little attention to Africa—and then only to its aberrant phenomena with little or no analysis. Éla teaches us how to read the signs of Africa's time, what kind of questions to ask, what sustained hope in the midst of desperation means, and also why African laughter itself is not only a celebration of life, but also a weapon of defense against tears.

SIMON E. SMITH, S.J.
AUGUST 1988

Notes

1. See *The Emerging Gospel. Theology from the Underside of History*, ed. S. Torres and J. Eagleson (Maryknoll, NY: Orbis, 1978).

2. Orbis, 1986.

3. *Voici le temps des héritiers* (Paris: Karthala, 1981); *L'Afrique des villages* (Karthala, 1982); *La ville en Afrique noire* (Karthala, 1983).

4. See, for example, F. Eboussi-Boulaga, *Christianity without Fetishes* (Orbis, 1984).

Preface

When Paul VI visited Kampala in 1969, he issued a challenge which has not been forgotten: "You may, and you must, have an African Christianity." And, indeed, this demand somewhat satisfies the deep hopes that now appear throughout research, colloquia, and diverse publications from Africa. In certain churches, the desire to root the gospel in local realities is becoming a fundamental option demanded by the proclamation of the Good News.[1] It is the major concern that inspires the entire episcopate of Africa,[2] and the motivation underlying numerous studies in theology, religious life, liturgy and catechesis.[3]

In fact, Christianity permanently confronts its peculiar contradictions; throughout the history of missions, it has long practiced a "deculturizing" control over African populations—forcing them brutally to sever their roots and lose their authenticity. Even today, after a hundred years of evangelization, these young forms of Christianity remain subject to the cultural tutelage of their mother churches. It is not surprising then that centers of reflection are forming in Christian circles to try to enhance the value of misunderstood or rejected cultures so that local communities can express their faith in their own unique way.

Understanding these studies is vital today as the inroads and ascendancy of externally imposed models threaten national identities. Cultural questions raised by the churches have become part of a larger historical movement seeking to preserve or revive indigenous creativity. Christianity must inculturate itself if it does not want to be perceived as an apparatus or an ideological "phase" of colonialism. If the churches are to rediscover the true originality of Christian universalism, they must take on the historical particularity of each people.[4]

From this perspective, isn't there a good reason to recapture the importance of a faith which strives to join the African in that relationship with the Ancestors which has always been central to daily life? Likewise, if local churches determine to narrate the story of salvation and to celebrate the mystery of faith in the style of an African *palaver*, the question of language must become a fundamental theme of study. Local communities searching for their future are the preferred place for such study, because faith must be lived in the contexts where Christians confront their own world each day.

The churches of Africa can no longer evade these basic questions. The research will be difficult, since a complexity of factors affect the African understanding and experience of faith and the gospel. First of all: Who should undertake the fundamental task of inculturation? Surely the initiative must not be left to men and women who have come from elsewhere, sometimes themselves disoriented by different cultural origins, education and background. They often fail to understand the relationship with the invisible, which perhaps constitutes the center of gravity in the African world. (The importance of this relationship is underlined by problems of sickness and healing and by the beliefs or practices of sorcery.)

How is Christianity to be "Africanized" when 70% of the missionaries are from Europe or North America? The question is serious, considering the slowness with which local communities mature. The responsibility of Africans is immense in this area, and the future of the African churches may depend on it. It is especially important in the training institutes where young people are being prepared to take up pastoral ministries in the villages and slums of Africa. It seems doubtful that the imitation of outmoded models currently being questioned in the older forms of Christianity allows young Africans undergoing training to become solidly equipped to confront specific pastoral problems in a socio-cultural context which requires a fresh examination of all revelation and Christian tradition.[5] The in-depth evangelization of Africa requires better preparation of men and women in the churches, and a new respect for local human resources. Nothing is more important and necessary today than centers for reflection and study. The tasks to be undertaken exclude any kind of improvisation; rather they require imagination and creativity that must be supported by in-depth studies.

The problem is further complicated by the fact that the current generation does not necessarily look to African cultural traditions for answers to all its questions. Because the young people of today have emerged from school systems conveying alienating messages and few have experienced initiation rites, the totality of the African universe is not open to them, and they cannot draw on the knowledge transmitted by the great masters of oral tradition. As a result, the meaning of the traditional ceremonies escapes them, and use of the oral style is barely discernible in their manner of speaking or living.

It is true that the socio-cultural environment defined by references to ancestral beliefs still often exercises control. Even in westernized cities, magic and sorcery are returning on a large scale. Despite the obstacles set up by colonization and the traditional methods of evangelization, African religions still manage to find a new vitality. We need only cite the return to traditional medicine. Surely all these areas where Africa is rediscovering itself attest to a deep crisis within changing societies. Awareness of this crisis should make us give up once and for all any mental picture of Africa as a stable world resistant to change, always the same, a stranger to time and history. We must fully recognize that cracks now appear in the "unanimity" postulated by colonial ideology. We will be no better than African antiquarians if we avoid or hide the challenges of our current history. True inculturation of the faith cannot make use of outmoded cultural forms.

In the areas of the church which reflect foreign customs brought from the outside, we must face up to the tensions and conflicts of contemporary society—conflicts which cause Africans to revitalize their traditions and reinterpret their past. Culture itself is a way of living that is continually challenged by the critical events which shape a people's history. Socio-political and economic processes that defy tradition continually adapt and change a culture. This rereading of the collective memory takes place in daily life, with all its conflicts and tensions. Conversion to this form of daily life can allow the church and the word of God to encounter living Africa in its own historical situation.

In order to restore authenticity to Africans, great importance should be given to the cultural factors that inspired the initial resistance to foreign control.[6] The supposition that the black world is incapable of popular mobilization is based on a naive vision of

African reality.[7] African forms of expression—images and songs, mocking words, attitudes born during peasant and worker struggles—refute the supposed passivity or resignation of the black peoples in the face of glaring injustices. The seeds of struggle and resistance that correspond to the genius of these peoples are concealed everywhere. Other ways of opposing the forces of oppression surge forth from the cultural depths.

Often resistance takes the indirect route of talk or of silence. The laughter and the humor of the black people are among the weapons of African culture. "To keep myself from weeping, I open my mouth and then I laugh."[8] This is not a lack of knowledge or resignation, but a tactical maneuver; according to ancestral wisdom, the panther should never be attacked from the front, but always from the rear. In certain African countries, a single word, a turn of phrase, or a song are enough to make a repressive regime unpopular. The art of mocking those in power is a form of struggle which shows that no one is taken in. Culture rediscovers its relevance in the backwoods and bars of a society where communication takes place underground. Understanding the contemporary reality of African culture and its powers of mobilization goes beyond rediscovering traditional beliefs and rites, customs and institutions. One must also go back to the silent language of a people who refuse to be silent in a muzzled Africa. The words and expressions of those "perched on high" are more or less understood. Africans have a way of capitalizing on an official speech, and using it to convey an alternate meaning to people within the society—a meaning often radically opposed to the official statement. The creation of this form of speech is the work of a culture perfectly integrated with the struggles of the people.

At a time when Africans, like other peoples, are facing the shock of technological and cultural modernity, *liberation of the oppressed must be the primary condition for any authentic inculturation of the Christian message.*[9] This is the central axis of the papers in this short book, which begins with the questions of faith posed by cultural variables, an internal dimension of the African's condition. In order to understand what is at stake, we need to place these matters in the overall context of a society and a history marked by conflicts—conflicts which lead to a rereading of our African memory. The basic issue of the credibility of Christianity is being raised from within the dynamic which allows Africans to escape from the inhumanity of the destiny to which certain factors would condemn them. Everything that specifically marks the Christian tradition today is questioned, if one watches those Africans who live in oppression and suffer under the injustice of ideological, social, political, and economic structures. To some degree, African culture has found asylum and refuge today among village peasants and city slum-dwellers. What must be deepened, though, if faith is to move ahead, is the ability of the gospel to respond to the situation that can no longer be covered up: "the powerful and almost irreversible aspiration that people have for liberation."[10] So critical reflection on the relevance of an African Christianity requires us to identify the structures or strategies of exploitation and impoverishment against which Africans have always struggled, finding their own specific forms of resistance within their cultures.

From this standpoint, we come up against the self-proclaimed innocence of certain church practices that pretend to ignore the mechanisms of domination in Africa. These very practices risk cutting us off from those gospel acts that are signs that Christ is the word of life in our daily existence, and that he intervenes with all the power of the cross in the tragic situation of our people. The challenge of poverty and oppression must be faced or else the process of "inculturating" the faith will become yet another excuse for inaction.

For older African generations, evangelized in the tradition of colonial Christianity, these perspectives mean wrenching changes and making decisive options for the future of local churches. Called to confess Jesus Christ in a continent which tends to become a veritable empire of hunger, perhaps we should rethink the whole question of understanding and experiencing faith. Our reflection must begin with the concrete practices and alternatives wherein the memory and the resistance of our people have been articulated. How to speak about God in the living conditions of the poor in African societies torn apart by many forms of neo-colonial violence? This is the question which should mobilize African churches.

My reflections here were born from practical experience among peasants faced with famine, drought, and sickness. For a long time, I was involved in the life of villages that had been crushed by the weight of deep injustices and frustrations. I was led to the difficulties and questionings of communities stirred by the Word of God. As I became their companion in their "little steps of liberation," I could no longer think about any aspect of faith without reassessing its impact on the future of marginalized peasants. In the midst of constraints and tensions, threats and misunderstandings, the gospel becomes a fountain of living water from which we can draw the strength to move ahead. It illuminates the great questions of existence and nourishes the hope of the poor. This reading of the gospel through the eyes of the little ones of the earth constitutes the background of my reflection.

I do not intend to propose a full treatise on theology. I am only presenting one fundamental theme with many variations, and trying to examine it thoroughly. I was called on to respond to many urgent requests involving the destiny of those "rejected by history." And so I have not had the time to step back from my pastoral involvement in order to pursue systematic research on the questions that have arisen out of my work with the peasants. I have had to limit myself to opening new paths and undertaking a limited approach to the problems that the gospel raises in the context of the people's struggle for survival. An uncomfortable and difficult experience! My time was parcelled out among work in the villages, outside interruptions, and the time-consuming visits of young people who required long periods of patient listening. In the evening I found myself exhausted by this itinerant ministry. The only time that remained for me to be with myself and sit down with myself at my "table of existence" was the night.

It is hard to write in the difficult conditions of life in the bush. The themes of this study were composed by the poor light of a gasoline lantern set on top of a thick dictionary and a Bible. I had no choice but to accept these rigorous conditions of life—which perhaps are integral to a "Third World theology." The requirements of faith in our societies do not always demand a life of luxury! What is important is to make a contribution to the debate that is beginning. A reflection carried out in a family spirit, stimulated by the daily confrontation with the problems of nascent communities, allows us to wake up to the life of the church, to its appeals, to its quest for better practice of its own mission. I had the happiness to see this meaning of the church being born as I examined with my working companions the reflections which came from our common experience.

May I be permitted here to thank the African nuns and the young black priest who brought me their fraternal support in the hard struggle, carried on day and night, to try to think and live an experience of liberating evangelization, "without gold or silver," with empty hands, in the midst of a church totally white and powerful. The birthplace of the reflections that run through this study was the villages of the lowlands and of the mountains where we went on foot, our only baggage a sleeping mat, a Bible, our heart, and the love of the poor.

A number of organizations, local churches, religious institutes, church groups, and intellectual circles have also given me the opportunity to share with them the questions that trouble me, to clarify them, and to examine together our options for the future. To all of them, I express my deepest thanks for the concern they brought to my effort to reflect critically on the questions of culture, liberation, and of the gospel that come today from the Africa of the little ones.

Notes

1. See A. Ngindu Mushete and others, *Combats pour un christianisme africain* (Kinshasa: Faculty of Catholic Theology, 1981).

2. See "Report on Africa of the Episcopal Conferences of All-Africa, at the 1974 Synod of Bishops, Rome" in *Modern Missionary Documents and Africa*, edited by Raymond Hickey (Dublin: Dominican Publications, 1982), pp. 209-245.

3. See in particular what is happening in Zaire, where the African church of tomorrow is perhaps being born today.

4. See C. Geffré, *Théologie et choc des cultures*, Colloque de l'Institut Catholique de Paris (Paris: Cerf, 1984).

5. *"Ad Gentes,"* no. 22, in *Vatican Council II: The Conciliar and Post Conciliar Documents*, edited by Austin Flannery (Northport, NY: Costello, 1975), pp. 839-840.

6. On the role of local cultures in liberation struggles, see Amilcar Cabral, *Unité et lutte* (Paris: Maspero, 1967).

7. For an insight into the importance of cultural factors in movements of protest and resistance during the colonial era, see A. J. Mbembe, "Pratiques culturelles et créativité populaire en Afrique Noire hier et

aujourd'hui," mimeographed, Toulouse, November 19, 1983.

   8. Quoted in *Le Messager*, 49 (November 20, 1984): 4.

   9. C. Geffré, in *Théologie et choc des cultures* (see note 4 above), pp. 10-11.

   10. Sacred Congregation for Doctrine of the Faith, *Instruction on Certain Aspects of the "Theology of Liberation,"* I (Boston: St. Paul Editions, 1984), p. 5.

Part I

Reawakening
the Wellsprings

Chapter 1

An Itinerary

As I write these lines, I realize the difficulty of translating an experience which merges with an itinerary—an itinerary of self-discovery on a road travelled with others, in the direction of Christ, toward whom all converges.

The Progression of the Mission and the Challenge of the Poor

Coming from a church born almost a century ago, a church that already shows signs of obsolescence, I find myself among the peasants of northern Cameroon. This encounter is a shock which is not only geographic and historical, but also religious. I am the son of a cocoa planter who was an avid reader of the Bible. We lived in a forest region which had been evangelized by Protestants and then, forty years later, by Catholics. I grew up in an atmosphere of struggles against forced labor, conscriptions for road work, and all the restrictive provisions of a colonial system. From a very young age—in spite of all prohibitions—I sang in my own language the music which became our national anthem in 1960. It had been composed by young students, many of whom came from my region. The birth of this music touched off a period in our history when the educated classes expressed their rejection of colonialism and claimed their rights as citizens.

Marked by the memory of these struggles, I find myself in a northern region affected by a state of invisible slavery, as the older priest, Baba Simon, explained on the night of my arrival. My first impression was that the people of the high country among whom I would live for many years are not merely rejected and bereft of decision-making power; they are also totally defenseless and deprived. The mountain peoples are poor because they have been exploited and oppressed for generations, *not* because they do not work.

For a quarter of a century, the non-Muslim peoples of northern Cameroon were down-trodden by an administration monopolized by aristocrats on horseback who had imposed their domination on the entire region. Not one single official in an executive position came from the mountain areas.[1] This systematic exclusion from decision-making is more serious in the villages and poor quarters where illiterate populations are subjected to a feudal system whose power is translated into various types of taxation and harassment. The peasants must undertake forced labor of all kinds, including roadwork, the construction of shelters to accommodate political and administrative meetings, and mandatory labor in the fields of the chief. Severe penalties are inflicted for refusing to work or for pilfering. Obligatory taxes are imposed to buy sheep for the chiefs during festivals. Traditional authorities do not hesitate to tax the peasants, in order to prevent health authorities from getting a foothold in the villages or to let children escape from attending school. Arbitrary imprisonment in the house of the chief of the canton is standard practice. Each year tax collection is a source of frequent abuse.

Equally serious is the risk run by mountain people who go down to the plain, only to return and find themselves without land. We often hear young farmers say: "They took my field away"; "The land no longer belongs to us"; "If I improve my land today, the authorities will come and take it tomorrow"; "We're despised; they take our land." This violence culminates in an agricultural system inherited from the colonial regime.

The crucial problem confronting the peasants each year is the conflict between cotton and millet. Cotton is grown for export to earn foreign exchange; millet is grown as food. "The peasant always loses when he grows cotton for sale; he would rather grow peanuts, millet, beans, peas—anything but cotton. But he hasn't got the power, because they take away his field to grow cotton, cotton which he doesn't want to grow." This system of production is perceived as a genuine form of exploitation. "You have worked to make another rich," declared a group of peasants.

Faced with this situation, I had to free myself immediately from a certain number of constraints in order to get a fresh perspective on the problems of my mission. I did not feel called to become the manager of a form of decaying Christianity, bound up in its doctrine and discipline, so I decided to keep my distance from a model of a church designed elsewhere by people who do not know the conditions of the mountain peoples. I had to refuse the false security available to someone who moves into another's house. I could never forget my experience in the south, where we had to close the churches and begin catechizing the people all over again. In order to capture the meaning of my mission, I *had* to live in insecurity. That led to radical questions: "What is the cutting edge of the gospel that can be most directly accessible and meaningful for these people? How shall we live our faith, and thus create around us a desire for the living God? Don't we have to convert ourselves before preaching conversion to others?" Everything impelled me to abandon the traditional Christian questions, and patiently let another language of the gospel burst forth from the life of the people.

This question of language forced itself on me whenever I encountered languages in which the Kingdom of God has yet not been proclaimed. How could I dare to express my faith in a culture marked by the civilization of the hills and millet? How could I find a Kirdi[2] "scripture" in the Word of God? This is the focus of my work. Before any experience of faith can be celebrated in community, we have to ask ourselves about symbols and gestures, the attitudes, and the translation of the message we use. Everything must correspond with the center of peoples' lives, taking into account their tradition and history.

We have to rethink the mystery of faith in reference to a culture "told by God to grow millet." Each year after the harvest we were questioned by peasants who were celebrating the festival of the "Beer of God"—a true thanksgiving in honor of God who provides the rain, the millet and good health, and protects people during the growing season. These agricultural ceremonies tied to the annual cycle of millet raise questions that must be answered within the heart of the communities closely linked to the mountain peoples.

The meaning of the festival, deeply rooted in the peoples' mentality and their socio-religious practices, forces us to reinterpret it as a response of faith to the message of the Beatitudes.

A serious question also arises about the celebration of Easter within the life of the local communities. Easter is no longer a time of submission to Christian duty; by assuming the values of culture, it becomes instead a celebration of the victory of life over death (1 Cor. 15:54-57). So the "gospel palaver" around the death of Jesus becomes an intensified moment in the lives of the communities which re-experience the narrative of the Passion through the difficulties of their daily life. The Bible, a calabash of sacrifice, and a cross are placed on a mat in front of the stone altar, recalling the life and ministry of Jesus of Nazareth. Gestures and attitudes express the feelings of the people gathered to witness the Passion of the Savior. Against a background of funeral chants for the dead, accompanied by a five-string guitar, catechumens in the final stages of instruction recall the crucifixion, moving around the altar to the rhythm of the women's lamentations. A large cross painted white, the color of death, is presented to the assembly; each one present comes and touches it to take on the strength of the Tree of Life whose "leaves can heal the pagans" (Rev. 22:2).

This search for appropriate symbols is linked to the life of the communities which are becoming aware of the problems in their villages, and are striving to end the structural injustice which colors their reading of the gospel. For it is precisely in their situation of sin and death that the power of the Risen One becomes real, the One who opens a way of hope for human beings. That is why Easter has become the most appropriate day to present a child to God. As in a traditional ceremony of consecration, infants are held up to the sun, the symbol of Jesus Christ, the true light of life.

No opportunity should be missed to translate the newness of the gospel. At every moment I must be alert for something new that can spring into life. I must constantly live with my ears pricked up to catch the faintest murmurs of the Spirit who speaks to the church in the context of the African.

The Sacrament of Community

The perspective of our mission is no longer to baptize as many people as possible, to count the number of Easter communions, to settle marriage problems, or to play, as priest, the role of a big shot in the village. I care little for the tangible results or the statistics of my work. It is not so much a matter of completing a list of tasks, as it is of being and living with the people, of finding them where they are. In every pastoral program I undertake, I ask myself: Does a community exist here? What must be done to help it come into being? Am I able to draw the people together by the way I'm living my faith? What are the essential concerns in the life of this village that can bring people together and help the gospel take root?

Everything begins with these questions. That takes time. In the villages the burden of my surroundings forces me to stop living by the clock and to respect the steps others take down their path to faith. In our mission, we must learn to wait and not move too fast. Sometimes the mission must be fulfilled with little outward show— with perhaps no baptisms for several years, if necessary. It is not essential that the church be full every Sunday, but that the gospel become a place of meeting and gathering which transcends the differences and confrontations among people.

Certain events force me to turn back to the Nazareth experience, to go to the heart of that time and to live it again, not as a time of pre-mission, but as the mission itself. That is not easy. It is much like crossing a desert. For a variety of reasons, many people will never be baptized or participate in the Eucharist; community is perhaps the only sacrament they can share. In it and around it, they are called to live out the values of the Kingdom. We should rejoice, then, at the birth of gospel communities where men and women take charge of their lives and their future.

The real liturgical problem in these mission contexts is knowing how to celebrate the birth and progress of these communities. If they are the places where faith roots itself in the daily experience of people, they can also be where an indigenous liturgy is created. Such a liturgy makes more sense than the pious repetition of old formulas. A good example is when there is a need for a celebration that conforms to a traditional ritual—such as the need to celebrate a woman's pregnancy or to ask for healing. These traditional rituals challenge Christian families in the new communities.

For me, the quest for suitable forms to express faith is always linked to an absolutely basic question: How can the gospel become the leaven which leads to a new meaning in life, but always with reference to Jesus of Nazareth who is, *par excellence*, both the

Other and one's closest neighbor? Even after meeting many different people, one concern still troubles me: How can I free each person I meet to truly encounter the Word of God and to become a vital part of God's ongoing creation?

From now on, we can no longer confine ourselves to "teaching doctrine," mouthing standard religious instruction in a catechumenate. Where people aspire to escape from misery and captivity, we must move from catechism to revelation. Recapturing the dynamic of faith acknowledges the reality of the community with all the fears paralyzing its ordinary life. That is why the people of the villages and slums are asked to examine their fears when they lay claim to the gospel to direct their lives. Our mission must stimulate the people's ability to act and struggle against misery, ignorance, and injustice. Its primary task is to develop communities that will shoulder the distress of other people who search for more in life.

Each occasion in the life of the village should be oriented around a theme. Thus each stage of the planting cycle can open a window to contemplate the God of the peasants—God the potter, God the worker, and God the shepherd of the people. Similarly the "friends of the gospel" must become aware of God's presence in the hut of the mother whose granary is empty. They must recognize God in the shade of the faidherbia trees where the thirsty peasant stops to recover his strength. We search for God through the voice of a people pleading for rain in time of drought. Then Jesus Christ appears as God with a peasant's black face and hands toughened by labor under the burning sun. Humanity is thus linked to the God of Revelation through its quest for food, and nothing can come between work and prayer.

In a society where ancestral religion still controls agriculture, Christianity must take into account the aspirations of men and women who need water and millet. But the Christian faith must also exist in an antagonistic civilization where the peasants know they are working so others may prosper. Naturally, they ask themselves what the Word of God says about the harvest. What can they do so that they can profit from the riches of their own work? The reference to the One who "offered himself as a sacrifice for our liberation" opens the way to understanding the relationship between sacrifice and meal, and to rediscovering the relevance of the Passion and Resurrection to the life of the villages. Thus our mission strives to re-create the community of the gospel by taking on the permanent challenges of oppression and injustice.

Christians cannot remain indifferent to the daily treatment of people. How can we experience God without becoming involved in these situations? Credible involvement, though, must go beyond acts of charity. It is no longer sufficient to bring a basket of provisions to people; rather, we must help them discover their ability to organize themselves to protect their fields and prevent arbitrary actions. One of our basic tasks is to show people their rights as citizens by translating into their languages the preamble to the Constitution, the fundamental law of our land. The illiterate peasants need to understand that their tax certificate (which illiterate citizens take to be a passbook) is also proof that they have the right to water, to roads, to electricity. When they become aware of these basic rights, they can challenge the administration to provide the services.

The first weapon of self-defense we give the communities is literacy training. Teaching the basic skills leads to reflection on the problems of health, nutrition, agriculture, and human rights. At the same time, the school is turned into the center of vitality of the community. A peasant once said: "A village without a school is a village of slaves." Everything we do is designed to convince the people that they can change their situation, and to restore their power to speak out. During a study session on the meaning of tax certificates, a peasant said, "We will die if they take away our right to speak."

By trying to share the destiny of the marginalized peasants, our mission concentrates on doing whatever it can to bring attention to the tragic situation of these people who were condemned long ago to ignorance, poverty and oppression. The ecclesial context, however, has carefully avoided some of these questions in order not to be sent packing. Conscientizing evangelization is not easy, partly because the church is sluggish to take a position, particularly at the level of pastoral agents who have many differing interests. This lethargy has surfaced during meetings held to discuss effective behavior for confronting regulations that victimize our communities.

It is much easier to dig wells or to provide primary health services than to face up to oppressive situations in the name of the gospel, or to rethink our mission in terms of the requirements of justice and equity. The proclamation of the Resurrection requires intelligible words and deeds in the reality of the people's history. Wherever violence reduces human beings to poverty and silence, the poor need witnesses who can follow Jesus in showing love "even to the end" (John 13:1). There is a certain risk in living our mission in the midst of a people who want to speak, to live freely, and to take responsibility for common concerns; but it is a requirement of faith that cannot be ignored without betraying the gospel. In 1983, Christian Tumi, archbishop of Garoua, said: "Wherever free people created in the image of God are oppressed, liberating them from all forms of oppression is a duty imposed on me by the gospel which frees from all slavery."

In order to proclaim this hope, we had to make a clear commitment to the landless peasants who are reduced to silence and marginalization, and subject to taxes of all kinds. Our mission implies an experience of solidarity with the powerless. The burning questions of an evangelization concerned with the structures of exploitation and injustice seem as distant as the Counter-Reformation from any doctrine whose cornerstone is catechetical instruction. Given this context, I feel the need to rediscover the resources of our African oral tradition in order to tell of the love of a God who gathers together and liberates. I must walk beside the African and complete with him the long course of traditional initiation in order to demonstrate the evocative power of the gospel. Rediscovery of communal dialogue, of talking and listening, becomes a privileged moment of mission. And the night becomes the best time for communication and mystery: word and gesture, rhythm and song, poem and game all fit together in a total experience of encounter. As we enter the socio-cultural framework of a people's memory, we try to invent paths to the future, beginning from actual questions.

Along this route, the traditional model of church dies. It is a church which gives the impression that it has nothing to say, either by the insignificance of its words or by its inattention to what is actually happening. The church that is established during this experience of mission is a church which becomes a part of peoples' lives; it struggles with them against misery and injustice. On every level of encounter with men and women, old and young, we need the courage to confront basic questions and to help people understand not only the present but also the future. In this way, we must make a special effort to keep in touch with the old sages, including those who tend to be thought of as sorcerers, for they have a message for us as well. Before the written word destroys our ability to listen and remember, we need to hear the voices of these older Africans who carry the message of a millennium-old Africa to new generations. They are our "catechists" who initiate us into the real life of the people. Contact with them is vital.

But we also need to keep our ears open to the young who search for new answers to the questions of life, family and marriage, birth and death. Our mission involves spending much time with the young people, the seed of the future. They must be our priority; experience with the young shows us how to develop solidarity between them and their people. Finally, in villages where the tribal court is important in regulating the problems of daily life, we must help the young to be heard.[3]

This approach to mission goes hand in hand with my rereading of the gospel and with my celebration of faith, starting with some hard questions as to how we can announce the Lord of Life to men and women who live in situations close to death. What is at stake is a pedagogy of faith that allows communities to resist the injustices surrounding them every day. This approach to faith is a long-lasting reflection coming to birth in the midst of violent systems of oppression.

As each community gathers under a tree to hear the Word of God and asks how its people can become the thinkers and architects of their own future, a true understanding of faith grows. We must enter their understanding of God's realities to grasp the meaning of revelation—beginning with topics that are usually considered secondary or of little importance. For it is precisely through questions of health, access to land, food, and the power to speak out that the conflict emerges—the conflict between hope and the meaninglessness of a life of poverty and slavery.

My reflection on faith is rooted in the beginning of my experience in the north. A theologian must stay within earshot of what is happening within the community so that community life can become the subject of meditation and prayer. In the end, a theologian is perhaps simply a witness and a travelling companion, alert for signs of God and willing to get dirty in the precarious conditions of village life. Reflection crystallizes only if it is confined to specific questions. But to get to the heart of the matter, reflection must also confront what is happening elsewhere; it must enlarge its field of reference. Thus a new era begins where the future is a common task. Shouldn't we place our bets today on a project for humanity, where the masses are no longer useless to the world? As Cheikh Hamidou Kane, the author of *The Ambiguous Adventure,* says:

> We have not had the same past, but—unquestionably—we shall have the same future. The era of individual destinies is over. Thus the end of the world has really arrived for each of us, for none can live any longer taking thought only for self-preservation.

On my journey, which begins with biblical discussions on faith in the villages of Africa, I can take different paths that intersect here and there around the world today. We encounter each other and even speak a common language, the language of humanity being liberated. Throughout the world, small groups work, each with its uniqueness and in its own way, taking "in its heart and on its shoulders the misery of the people; not like a stranger, but as equals, involving them in the struggle for their own deliverance," in the words of Father Lebret. If we ignore the most important values to which Africans cling, how can this quest come to its proper conclusion?

Notes

1. According to the testimony of Monsignor Tumi, archbishop of Garoua, testimony confirmed by a number of observers, the situation in the former northern province has greatly changed since Paul Biya came to power as president. An event without precedent in the political history of the country has taken place! A genuine son of the mountains, J. B. Baskonda, has just entered the government. He is one of those youths taught by Baba Simon to take pride in being Kirdi.

2. *Kirdi* means "pagan" in the Fulfulde language spoken by the Fulani ethnic group. Since their *jihad* of the late eighteenth and early nineteenth centuries, the Muslim Fulani have applied the term generally to a large number of other northern Cameroonian peoples who fled and refused to accept Islamic beliefs.

3. To mark the importance of young people in the life of the mission, I built the Foyer Aimé-Césaire as a place of life and reflection for the students of Tokombéré.

Chapter 2

The Ancestors
and Christian Faith

The subject of this chapter—the relationship between the ancestors and the Christian faith—is meaningless for a form of Christianity that merely transfers dogmas, rites, rules, and customs formed overseas for African traditions, which are then violently cast off. But discussion of this relationship becomes a very important question for a faith that can accept, with discernment, all the signs of an existing culture. Of course, such openness requires an effort to purify and liberate.

In this respect, the famous dispute of the 17th century over Chinese rites is still a paradigm that clarifies the difficulties posed by a form of Christianity identified with a particular civilization. During the 17th century, Catholicism was almost wholly identified with Western civilization. The work of Matteo Ricci and his Jesuit colleagues to take on aspects of Chinese culture collided with the phenomenon of European ethnocentricity. A church that is not able to free itself from its contingent social structures cannot be open to the universal in the experience of life.

If the past does indeed shed light on the present, we need to rethink the Christian message today; otherwise it will become one more disturbing influence in Africa, at a time when Africans, who refuse to part with their cultural identity, confront an irrupting foreign civilization bent on conquest. This is the vital context of our discussion. How can we live and express our faith so that it be-

13

comes more than an alienating reflection of a foreign world which attacks our indigenous customs and beliefs? How can we live our faith so it will not marginalize and discredit our ancestors? Posing this question in very practical terms, when the elders of newborn Christian communities reproach the young for having forgotten the dead, we must ask ourselves as Christian leaders how the gospel regards the cult of the ancestors. If we are willing to take into account the concrete reality of each of our diverse peoples with their basic human hopes and problems, this same question has to be radical. Can the church become the place in black Africa where communion with the ancestors is possible? These questions suggest several areas for reflection.

African Symbolism

First of all, an important general observation. In traditional black Africa, the dead are almost always honored in some way according to the funeral ceremonies used by a particular ethnic group. In many traditional societies, the cult of the dead is perhaps that aspect of culture to which the African is most attached—the heritage clung to above all else. Indeed, the cult of the ancestors is so widespread throughout Africa that it is impossible to avoid the questions this practice raises for Christian life and reflection. In some countries the cult of the ancestors is formally recognized by the government. At official receptions in Zaire, for example, the first toast is always proposed in honor of the ancestors and a few drops are poured on the earth where the ancestors lie.

Veneration of the ancestors takes many forms according to each different African society. But what is the fundamental structure of the cult of the ancestors in black Africa, its underlying intentions, its key ideas? Basic to it are the signs which influence and envelop the lives of Africans, constantly recalling the presence of the ancestors in the warp and woof of their existence. One such sign is the new name given during initiation to adulthood. The ceremony of initiation is more than a language of gestures and symbols; it is a decisive experience that changes the initiants' state of being, granting them a mode of existence in the larger world of the ancestors.

Another sign is the family vault where those who have died over several generations lie together in the very space where life continues. In the African way of thinking, a grave is where the presence of the invisible is concentrated. Burial places where the ancestors lie are sacred spots where they can be approached with offerings and consulted in times of crisis. Among the Bantu, the most solemn oath is the one made over a grave.

African art serves the cult of the ancestors; well-known is the role of statues and masks in the great majority of African societies. We now understand that these objects are not "fetishes," as collectors of exotic art first led Europeans to believe. Statues and masks are representations on a human and not a divine level of the spiritual presence of the ancestors. They are not worshipped. The symbols which often appear on the statues of ancestors reflect the power of each one. Their deeds encourage and stimulate their descendants, and thus establish a genuine solidarity in time among the generations. Similarly, the African mask has an evocative power which dramatizes the presence of the ancestors among the living. In other societies, certain ethnic groups like the Bamileke bury a skull of an ancestor under the bed and regularly offer libations to it. Elsewhere an altar is set up for parents and grandparents.

Among the mountain peoples of northern Cameroon, where the cult of the ancestors is highly developed, each head of family possesses a jar which represents his father or grandfather. This jar is often called *Baba*, the same word with which a man addresses his father while alive. It is surprising to see the level of spirituality achieved by these apparently very uncultured people, from whom one might expect less polished practices. Their cult is not devoted to tombs or even skulls, but to a purely symbolic element. The soul of the deceased resides in the empty jar, which is most often placed under the millet granary that is the heart of the mountain home, giving the ancestors a privileged place in precisely that spot. If you happen upon one of these jars and ask the head of the household what it is, he will answer without hesitation, "That is my father" or "That is my grandfather." No rite involving the ancestors is possible without the existence within the family group of what the Mada of northern Cameroon call the *pra*. This word denotes both the jar representing the ancestor and the cult which is offered. Only with the *pra* is it possible to have a prayer, a libation, a sacrifice, or a celebration of the festival of the ancestors. But the funerary jar is not merely a necessary condition for any liturgy involving those who have died, it also expresses the African understanding of death.

Many African cultures will never say that a person has died, but rather that one has departed, one has left us, one is no longer, one has passed on.[1] For the African, death is not the annihilation of a being. Strictly speaking, one is not afraid of death; but what one does fear is dying without leaving children behind. The absence of sons is the worst curse for the black African. This obsession with having children reveals a deep concern—descendants are needed to fulfill the ultimate responsibility of maintaining the cult of the ancestors. It is terrible to die, after having broken the ties of family, clan, and community. Africans fear dying without leaving someone behind who "will remember them"; they fear dying "without a community to which they will be attached."[2] Without a cult offered for them, the dead are condemned to wander, deprived of all communication with the living. Hence the importance of the funerary jar which manifests a vital communion with the ancestors. Because it actualizes the presence of the deceased, it is the basic sign that clarifies this central affirmation of African thought: "*The dead are not dead*!" The ancestor's jar concretely testifies to this nearness of the invisible—the invisible which is perhaps a center of a gravity, holding together the African religious universe. The *pra* functions as a symbol, therefore, binding together things that seem distant. It is a means of overcoming the distance and the oblivion created by death, and it creates a bond of unity between the living and the dead.

Among the so-called "pagan" peoples of northern Cameroon, the omnipresent funerary jar has a truly revelatory function. It is a symbol whose purpose is to put one in touch with the ancestors. When the Mada pray over the *pra*, they speak as if they are really talking to an actual person, for it establishes a true channel of communication between the being symbolized and the person entering into contact with that being. The *pra* is a vital bond that permits the ancestors to communicate with the living and to exercise their immediate and direct influence.

In order to understand the structure of the ancestor cult, we must turn again to the importance of symbolism. To Africans, the cult of the ancestors is inseparable from their overall vision of human beings and society. The cult lies within the context of kinship, which undergirds every sector of traditional African society.[3] Kinship can be defined as a vast working system that organizes individuals into a coordinated network of mutual actions and reactions. This background clarifies the ensemble of relationships and attitudes characterizing the communion in Africa between the living and the dead.

An understanding of kinship also provides a vision of the world in which human beings are intended to transcend earthly limitations. The key moments in the cult of the ancestors maintain the communal ties that bridge the crevasse of death. In a society where everything is within a sacred cosmic order, the ancestors are remembered at the critical moments in the life of a person or the community. Birth, marriage, agricultural festivals—all are integrated through the coherence of the traditional society where human beings are in communion with the powers of nature and are defined by their relationship to God and to the ancestors. The profound meaning of the cult of the ancestors becomes clear when it is placed in the context of the African family, which is the foundation of its culture. Thanks to the kinship system, the ancestors remain linked to their families and continue to protect the living, caring for them and acting as their intermediaries, while receiving their respect, reverence, and solicitude.

It is important to note as well that while the cult of the ancestors maintains communion with the dead, it also reinforces ties among the living. Thus the Festival of the Bull, the *Maray*, celebrated in honor of the ancestors among the mountain peoples of northern Cameroon does not have a solely sacrificial meaning; it is also very important to the social life of the community. At the time of this festival, each district invites "the whole mountain" to share in its festivity. Thus all communities are able to visit each other in turn, going into every hamlet. Young and old alike are joined in one feeling of communion that reinforces the unity and cohesion of the entire ethnic group. To focus solely on the sacrifice itself overlooks an essential feature of mountain life. For in the sacrificial meal shared by each family member, a living communion is realized, which unites the different groups derived from a common ancestor. The Festival of the Bull goes to the heart of the belief in the ancestors and also reveals and maintains the power of the head of the family. While God is usually offered no more than a sheep, the

Festival of the Bull requires the sacrifice of an ox: It is a matter of bringing about the most important communion wherein each person finds a reason to be and to live.

Living in Christ Our Relationship with the Dead

Considering the importance of the cult of the ancestors and its structure within African society, we must now turn to the real issue for Christians: Is there any place in our life in Jesus Christ for maintaining a relationship between the living and the dead? Or must Africans break their relationship with their ancestors if they are to be converted to the gospel?

The ancestors have not yet found a secure place within the life of African Christians because missionaries have tended to confuse the ancestors with "spirits." A belief in spirits, a form of superstition, is incompatible with the Christian faith. As a result, the "cult of the ancestors" has been seen as a variation of the "cult of the spirits," a general phrase that includes different forms of animism. It has been presumed that the African wished to please the *Manes* (the spirits) of the ancestors so the ancestors would not harm them. In this view, the dead are likened to malevolent spirits that must be appeased by sacrifice; thus fear of the spirits appears to lie at the root of the "cult of the ancestors."

However, this interpretation ignores the overall structure of the bonds that unite the living and the dead, as well as the ritual behavior that characterizes the relationship with the ancestors. The Mada of northern Cameroon do not preserve the *pra* out of fear of their fathers, but out of the need to stay in communion with them and to bring them into the life of the family. Because the cult of the ancestors is such an integral part of the millet-growing civilization, it is inconceivable that a head of family would prepare beer from newly harvested millet and *not* share it with his ancestor, the father who bequeathed him the land. In any celebration involving beer, the head of the household always pours some on the earth for the ancestor. A similar relationship is evoked by a ceremony for newborns in which the child is first presented to the sun, a symbol of God and the source of life. The child is then placed under the protection of the ancestors.

None of these actions is inspired by fear of evil spirits. Even if "spirits" in the African context is equivalent to an actual symbol of evil, the belief in the ancestors springs from a different concept of existence and the universe. In Africa the dead are part of the family. As such, they do not represent hostile "powers" whose harmful influences must be neutralized by magical rites. Neither are they excluded from happenings in the life of the clan; rather, their presence is authentically experienced as the participation of the invisible world in the world of the living. So the libations and food offered to them are signs of respect and of fraternity in a cultural context where communication with the invisible is just one aspect of the total reality of people's lives. In other words, the deceased— and by that token, death itself—are integrated into the system of relationships that the living maintain with nature, family, and society. Drink and food offered to the ancestors are symbols, therefore, of the continuity of the family and of this permanent contact. In the African mind, these offerings express an attitude that is unchanged by death, which is the passage into the invisible. Accordingly, the African always behaves as if the ancestor were still living. Offering one's dead father a meal is a simple act of filial piety.

Over the years, what is no more than an anthropological reality has been too quickly labeled as "pagan" or "idolatrous." This serious misunderstanding must be resolved. Although I use the word "cult" in describing the respect paid to the ancestors, I specifically rule out the meaning this word has in the mind of many Christians. Indeed, "cult" is a term incorrectly applied in the African context where people express, through a relationship of community, the respect due the founders of the clan. In the strict sense, the word "cult" should not be used to describe a family relationship. When people offer beer and food to the dead, they understand perfectly well that they are not "performing a cult" to the dead, but instead reliving a kinship relationship with them, actualizing such a relationship once again in the living present. It is important to understand clearly that this is not a religious act, but rather a form of symbolic experience. Mbiti correctly asserts: "When these acts are directed towards the living-dead, they are a symbol of fellowship, a recognition that the departed are still members of their human families, and tokens of respect and remembrance for the living-dead."[4]

It is important to return to the African concept of death in order to understand the fundamental meaning of the word "cult" which I am using throughout—primarily for lack of a better word to refer to the ancestors. But it is also important to refer to the significance of African symbolism I have described above. Finally, we must also consider the relationship between the living-dead within the kinship system. All of these factors indicate that we should separate any idea of religion from the cult of the ancestors. Again, as Anselme Titianma Sanon observes, "Cult among us (Africans) connotes a dramatic celebration to summon a spirit or invisible being, which could be completed by the sacrifice of an animal such as a chicken or a goat. No idea of adoration or veneration slips into it—contrary to a current Christian notion."[5] Therefore, if the relationship with the ancestors consists of the belief that the deep communion established among the members of a family is not broken by death, but is maintained despite and beyond death, then nothing in this relationship is contrary to the Christian faith. In that case, is the head of a household in northern Cameroon allowed to keep the jar which represents his grandfather and to make those offerings which are dictated by tradition?

Some Vatican pronouncements that bear on this question include the decisions on the Chinese rites and the ceremonies to honor Confucius (December 8, 1939), the Japanese rites (May 26, 1936), and the Malabar rites (April 9, 1940). The controversies surrounding these rites led to a statement of general principles and rules of conduct that are relevant here. To clarify policy for missionaries, the Sacred Congregation for the Propagation of the Faith reminded the faithful of the distinction between an element of culture that does not of itself constitute an obstacle to the purity of the faith, even if it is of religious origin, and a rite of strictly religious character that may well be incompatible with the requirements of the gospel. Hence it is wrong for Christians to condemn customs that are part of a civilization and that, in reality, have no bearing on religious life. In the case of the Chinese rites and Confucian ceremonies, Rome established a distinction between acts whose goal is religious and acts carried out to show "the honor due to a distinguished person according to ancestral traditions." An even more explicit distinction must be made between a cult which is the expression of a religion and a "respect which may be regarded as exclusively civil."[6] But I have already shown that we must avoid characterizing as a "cult" the offerings and libations that are above all marks of filial piety.

What does the church think of our African heritage? What is really at stake here is the idea of the family. In his "Message to Africa" of 1967, Paul VI continued the themes of the well-known instruction issued in 1659 by the Congregation for the Propagation of the Faith.[7] Paul VI expressed his respect for the traditional values of the African continent, and emphasized the "sense of family" and the "respect for the part played by the father of the family and the authority he has." In certain African civilizations, the Pope added, the father of the family "has a typically priestly function assigned to him whereby he acts as a mediator not only between the ancestors and his family, but also between God and his family, performing acts of worship established by custom."[8] Why, then, should Africans not include as part of their Christian faith this sense of family with all its implications and dimensions? For, in Africa, the invisible is as real as the visible; the two are inseparable, and communicate with each other through appropriate symbols.

The Role of Sacrifice and the Diviner

In various African societies sacrifices are offered *to* the ancestors. Such sacrifices regularly involve a blood offering, with various prayers and invocations; at the end there is a shared eating or "communion" of the "noble parts" of the animal.[9] Such a sacrifice is never offered without consulting a diviner who, in some ethnic groups, may be a blacksmith belonging to an untouchable caste. In cases of misfortune—sickness, a poor harvest of millet, drought, sterility of a couple, death of a wife or child, any kind of failure, or successive deaths in the family—the diviner often attributes these sad events to a misdeed, usually the failure to maintain relationships with the dead. A visit to a diviner will show how ordinary disturbances—briefly those relating to the fertility of land or people or the health of children—are events that can be equated with negligence in carrying out one's duty toward the dead. The diviner will show, for example, that the father-ancestor is causing the sickness of a child, and that he is asking for food. The diviner then prescribes offering the ancestor a certain type of food.[10]

It is easy to see how this type of situation can cause conflicts between the Christian faith and African tradition. Nevertheless, it is important to note that if the ancestor is offered a sacrifice of atonement, it is because he represents the symbolic face of the father who knows all, who punishes and who rewards. The teachings of the family, the tribe, and the culture are all crystallized in the life of the ancestor. In black Africa, the ancestors exercise a genuine control of society as the authentic guardians of tradition. Thus, restoring the order of the relationship between the living and the dead is also restoring the natural order of things. Belief in the ancestors as representatives of fatherhood plays a primordial role in African medicine, given the African understanding of sickness.[11] But the sacrifice offered to the ancestor as a token of atonement is in no case an act of "adoration."

For the mountain people whose lives are the source of my reflection, true religion is the sacrifice to God. For in this society, even though the belief in the ancestors is deeply rooted in custom, this belief does not overshadow their coherent monotheism—which forces us to question our stereotypes about that vague and convenient term of "animism." God remains the Lord of heaven and earth. During group prayer, the elders turn to God when seeking the fruits of creation and, in particular, that "freshness" which is so important to religious thought among the mountain people.

The basic importance of millet in the life of the Cameroonian people in the north is emphasized by their many rites, and their important seasonal sacrifices. First comes the festival of sowing when God is asked to grant rain. Then at the time of the harvest and its wasteful celebration, the people celebrate the *ouzom i Jegla*, the "Beer of God," the festival of thanksgiving to God for the new harvest. But God never yields before the power of the ancestors. Even though the ceremonies are organized in honor of the deceased members of the family, it cannot be said that the cult is addressed to the ancestors instead of to God. The ancestors do not replace the divinity, to whom everything is brought. For these reasons, it is more accurate to speak of the heads of family as mediators, even into the other world.

Herein lies an essential trait of African mentality that is shown even in the smallest matters. When a message is to be sent, one does not directly address the person involved—even if that person is present; one addresses a third party. Some observers have not realized this device, and have wrongly concluded that Africans believe in a divinity, but do not allow the divinity to intervene in daily life; they believe that Africans reserve such intervention for the ancestors.

Indeed, God is rarely the subject of sacrificial prayers, other than during the great seasonal sacrifices and times of calamity. God is addressed from time to time during the stress of difficulties in traditional daily life. From this observation, it is a short but quick step to conclude (and quite wrongly) that the "cult of ancestors" is *the* African religion, so much so that people thought that the God of Africans is a distant God who does not intervene in human affairs. Perhaps it is time to revise the many theories held about the role of the God-in-the-Sky in Africa. Among the native peoples of the savanna and forest, God is closer to human reality than was thought in the past. Under no circumstances are the ancestors ever placed on a divine plane, which could be used to justify sacrifices given to them. Thus the sacrifice offered to atone cannot be considered idolatrous; instead, it is a recognition of the authority of the ancestor, who guarantees the order of the world and judges moral life from the beyond.

Finally, what are we to think of the intervention of a diviner in this sacrifice? Are we to reject the sacrifice because the practice seems strongly anchored in village thinking? The diviner has always been persecuted by missionaries. To them, he represented the incarnation of African superstitions and paganism. The actual place of the diviner in traditional African society is much more serene and also more exacting. In the words of an ethnologist, divination "appears to be in fact the true 'total phenomenon.' It permits a concrete understanding of conflicts within family and society, as well as the anxieties and tensions arising from the religious realm. It spontaneously reveals as well people's concept of the ideal organization of their society while displaying their concept of the supernatural."[12]

With this global approach, it is not possible to reduce the work of the diviner to a purely religious phenomenon. The real question is not to decide whether Africans must cut off their relationships with the ancestors because they use diviners when offering sacrifices.

Rather, we must inquire how they can celebrate *as Christians* the relationships with the dead in a universe—an African universe—that has its own techniques, its theory of knowledge, its way of interpreting reality, its system of rationalization and explanation. More precisely, how can Africans live their faith in a socio-cultural world where everything that happens has an inner meaning which must be deciphered? The events of daily life always have a meaning related to belief in the ancestors. Therefore reality must be "decoded," starting with the different signs that manifest it. In the context of African culture where the ancestors are familiar with family events, what meaning is given to reality by a faith which lives in relationship with the dead? The techniques of divination raise this basic question for us. The proposal to recognize the cult of the ancestors in African Christian communities encounters socio-historical obstacles that are really quite peripheral to the meaning of the cult itself.

Christian Life and the Transformation of African Society

Ethnologists are increasingly aware that it is unusual to find an African society whose activities are undisturbed by change. What will happen to the Festival of the Bull tomorrow in northern Cameroon? Belief in the ancestors is also threatened by increasing urbanization. How many city dwellers really believe that the ancestors help them in their daily lives? There are no more reassuring certainties on this point. The results of research conducted by Raymond Deniel in Abidjan, capital of the Ivory Coast, for example, show that young people distance themselves from traditional customs or are even unaware of them.[13] Will sacrifices continue to be offered to the ancestors to ensure abundant harvests? Or will the harvest depend more and more on new cultivation techniques? How can the traditional cultural inheritance be maintained in Christian practice as African society changes? There is no doubt that the society is in flux, affected by the impact of events; a movement of simultaneous destruction and rebuilding results. How can we overcome the contradictions between the desire to be faithful to sound customs, and to be open to changes that are turning traditional society upside down?

Today many Africans, even those who are uprooted, refuse to

live their faith in a pattern borrowed from others. As a result, there is a great need to rediscover within Christianity an African vision of humanity—which is precisely what is at stake in dealing with the cult of the ancestors. We can gain guidance from a very close look at people in societies less brutally and rapidly disturbed by change, people who remain faithful to the cult of the ancestors while living the gospel.

In either case, the Vatican decisions previously cited give us substantial freedom in interpreting the acceptability of cultural traditions. We can begin with the important communiqué of February 28, 1941, from the Congregation for the Propagation of the Faith to the apostolic delegate in China: "The composition of a listing of permissible or forbidden ceremonies is to be absolutely avoided, . . . so as not to fall back into casuistic discussions which would revive past disputes in a different way." The declaration insists that there shall be no stooping to "specific details of the particular rites." And finally, in a key sentence, the last decision is left to conscience: "Priests and laypeople of good will shall be free to follow their own conscience in particular cases."[14] This teaching frees us from any scruples that might arise from the strangeness of customs and practices that prevail among non-Western societies.

In a declaration of October 17, 1935, the bishops of Madagascar issued the following directives, which I feel are still relevant: "Forbid customs which attribute to the dead a power over the living; accept signs of respect and thanksgiving directed towards the dead. No currently existing custom is formally forbidden as such, with the understanding that all customs are to evolve in a Christian direction."[15] These guidelines open up broad possibilities in defining a pastoral strategy responsive to local problems; it is not necessary, therefore, for me to propose ready-made recipes that will cover all situations.

We should emphasize, however, that in black Africa, belief in the ancestors is so closely linked with numerous aspects of traditional society that its abandonment will provoke widespread social crises. Belonging to the same *pra* reinforces the cohesion of the ethnic group. A Christian who abruptly abandons sacrifices to the ancestor is in danger of jeopardizing the unity of the entire clan. A Christian, therefore, must always consider the others who do not follow the Word of God, and, in particular, must always respect the head of the clan. It is wrong for a Christian to suddenly cut oneself off from people within the clan or to renounce the bonds of kinship.

Perhaps a study of the communion, lived in faith, of black Africans with their ancestors could benefit Christianity in the West, where a deep crisis centers on death, which is rapidly replacing sex as the most important taboo. In certain places today, cremation is the mark of a society that refuses to accept death or, when it cannot avoid death, minimizes it. Cremation is seen as the ultimate escape from the cult of cemeteries and the dead. Perhaps today's cult is no more than a reversion to archaic practices, which will ultimately decline along with these primitive modes of thought. In the meantime, the dead disappear under the flowers.[16]

Shouldn't the church profit by encouraging African Christians to stay in contact with their loved ones who have left this life, rather than by attacking our ideas about the ancestors? Of course, not everything is perfect in this relationship with the ancestors. The cult of the ancestors in black Africa, like everything else, needs to receive the good news of salvation in Jesus Christ; but it is precisely by accepting the cult that the church can purify it, transfigure it, and preserve it.

An African Style of Celebration

Restoration of community bonds with the invisible world is one of the fundamental tasks of that "African Christianity" which Paul VI launched at Kampala.[17] However, good ideas and logical doctrines are no longer sufficient; they must be incorporated into theology, catechesis, and liturgy. The Second Vatican Council opened up the possibility for young churches to explore liturgical and theological pluralism, which allows us to try certain experiments which could be fruitful for all of Christianity. Why should the mountain people of northern Cameroon break their *pra*s only to see them replaced by Christian relics on altars? If they find that the *pra* is a superstition that must be rejected to enter the church, won't the mountain people make the same judgment about the use of relics? In the mountains, the *pra* of the father is respected; in African churches, the bones of some unknown person, placed on the altar stone, appear to be a kind of fetish. Since, traditionally, there can be no prayer to the ancestors without the object which represents them, why shouldn't African Christians be permitted to bring the *pra* to a gathering in memory of the ancestors?

The liturgical introduction of the Feast of All Souls on November 2 certainly has not solved all the problems of the cult of the ancestors for African Christians. We need to find a new way to celebrate the day of the departed in our communities and have the heads of families play a major role that will also conform with tradition. Traditional African custom also prescribes commemorative funeral ceremonies each year; when the mountain people celebrate these festivals, each head of household prepares wine for the ancestors. Why can't Christians live out their faith in this context? Must they celebrate two commemorative festivals each year—one dictated by the official church calendar; and the second in the context of traditional life, only now with reference to Jesus Christ? In other words, should the church canonize the traditional African ritual of commemorative festivals? Or will it simply maintain a parallel calendar? These questions remain to be answered.

At the same time, increasing the number of Masses for the dead may not be a sufficient response of the church to all the aspirations of the African soul, with its deep desire to live in communion with the ancestors. We should take into account the unfortunate experiences introduced by the church, especially since the Middle Ages, when the cult of the dead tended to overwhelm the liturgy of the living, and to corrupt it by turning the Mass into a profit-making enterprise. Above all, we must avoid a situation in which practically all the Masses in a week are devoted to the memory of some deceased relative, so that a normal liturgical life is impossible for the contemporary community. African people need a cult which is not just a convention, but one which is an integral part of family life and is used when they need to call upon the ancestors.

Celebrated in this context, the Eucharist would express the mystery of the faith by signs marked by local customs. The structure of African prayer with its proper rhythm would be rediscovered and would replace the recitation of ready-made prayers. Furthermore, people's eyes would no longer focus only on the beyond, while remaining indifferent to present realities. On the contrary, prayer would be truly linked to the whole life of the gathered family. And this incarnate prayer would emphasize the importance of the name of the ancestor. The name would not be spoken by the celebrant, but preferably by the heads of the respective families, who would be trained for this "ministry" in their local communities. This is really a question of the style with which the mystery of salvation should be celebrated. The liturgy should reflect the requirements both of liturgical renewal, and also of a genuine encounter with the values of non-Christian religions.[18] It is hardly necessary to demonstrate the need and urgency for this research in all those countries where Christianity has always been linked to cultural expressions copied from the Roman liturgy—even down to the smallest detail.

The Ancestors and the Veneration of the Saints

Above all, we should not think for a minute that veneration of the saints can be an African substitute for communion with the ancestors! That would be just one more way to lead converts away from an essential dimension of their culture. It would be a dangerous mystification to give Africans the impression that the saints are now their ancestors, and that the saints alone are to be venerated and addressed in prayer. Sooner or later the converts would rediscover what ecclesiastical pressures had obliged them to suppress. If the church does not recognize the cult of the ancestors, people will be forced to practice it in secret. Even in "popular catholicism," as Abbé Pannet has demonstrated, the cult of saints—with its calendar, devotions, sanctuaries, pilgrimages, festivals both religious and secular, and its representations in art—is too marked by the historical experience of European Christianity for it to fully absorb the values of the African tradition.

The veneration of the saints is often a popular cult which has welled up from the spiritual depth of the people in a certain Christian region. Their knowledge of the saints is based less on precise hagiographical data, than on more or less anachronistic legends ascribing particular virtues and powers to the saints, and creating an image for their visual representation. A saint's name is chosen for a baby when it is baptized. The character of the patron saint may have little to do with this choice, but the saint's festival is always celebrated by the person who bears the saint's name. Even though the Council of Trent has said, "It is good and useful to invoke the saints with humility, . . . to rely on their prayers, their help and their assistance,"[19] the faith of the African still cannot be confined within the forms of a popular cult which is too characteristic of a particular epoch, a society, and a culture. Today, when

Africans search for their identity, the question is not to imitate a particular saint from the Roman calendar, but to situate the ancestors within the mystery of the Christian faith.

A New Language for the Gospel

Finally, how are we to think of the ancestors while trying to find a new way to read the gospel, a way organically related to an experience of community that seeks itself and creates itself? Every proposal related to the ancestors—the offerings and libations, the annual ceremonies for the dead, and ways of communicating with them—depends on this radical question which demands a fresh look at the gospel and at tradition. But Vatican II reminded us that "those who have not yet received the Gospel are related to the People of God in various ways."[20] Put another way, those who have not yet received the fullness of revelation and faith are to no lesser degree a part of the church, but in a way that is not historically visible. Of all those whom we Africans consider as our ancestors, who among them died alienated from God? And what "pagan" Kirdi has failed in his life to offer a sacrifice to God? For an African to be clothed with the dignity of an ancestor implies that one has constantly excelled in the practice of virtue. It would seem that the liturgy invoked on November 1, the Feast of All Saints, also includes all those pagan ancestors who, as we say in the Fourth Eucharistic Prayer, "searched for God uprightly." Haven't their hearts been mysteriously touched by that grace which goes beyond the sacraments? The same text of Vatican II says that "those who, through no fault of their own, do not know the Gospel of Christ or his Church, but who nevertheless seek God with a sincere heart, and, moved by grace, strive in their actions to do his will as they know it through the dictates of their conscience—those too may achieve eternal salvation."[21] The ancestors cannot be totally withdrawn from the action of the Word which "enlightens every one that comes into the world."

We may thus include the ancestors among those Christians "according to the Word," to use the words of St. Justin the Apologist.[22] But no serious reflection on whether or not they are saved is possible, unless we keep in mind not only the Word, but, above all, the one that is "beyond the Word"[23]—that is, the Holy Spirit at work in the universe. In this perspective, faith causes us to contemplate our pagan ancestors as part of that "great multitude from every nation, from tribes and peoples and tongues" that no one can number (Rev. 7:9). Can we exclude the old sages of Africa from those in the world below, to whom the resurrected Jesus announced the good news of salvation (I Pet. 3:19-20)? African Christians must not be limited to invoking the "saints," most of whom are unknown to them. Rather, based on our experience of communion with the ancestors, we must rethink the mystery of the church as a total communion with those ancestors who are not gods, but mediators of that life and those blessings that come from God alone. A true understanding of All Saints' Day requires inclusion of saints who have not been canonized or recognized by the ecclesial institution. In our African context, we must emphasize the phrase "all the dead *whose faith thou alone knowest*" (Fourth Eucharistic Prayer). A church which includes Abel the Just along with the sacrifices of Abraham and Melchizedek in its official Eucharistic Prayer (the First) cannot exclude our ancestors from its memorial. To experience in an African way the mystery of communion in Christ in whom is all that is visible and invisible (Eph. 1:10) is to incorporate our living relationship with the ancestors as a dimension of our total faith. The communion of saints thus includes communion with the ancestors.

If it has not always been this way, it is for purely historical or accidental reasons. Christianity was born during persecutions; the first Christians saw their own fathers die before their eyes and many others thrown into prison and tortured. Under these circumstances, it was nearly impossible to turn back to a cult of ancestors. The cult of ancestors was too involved in idolatry, and—do not forget—pagans persecuted Christians. Thus the church was built on the foundation of its own dead, who were venerated even more because they were the primary witnesses or "martyrs" of the faith. This context of persecution blocked the church from ever reevaluating the cult of the ancestors as it then existed. Christians became a new family in which the cult of the martyrs was substituted for the cult of the dead.

In the West today, the cult of ancestors will progressively dwindle from year to year to the extent that veneration of the saints further develops in the church and society becomes more secular. Perhaps today the Feast of All Souls represents nothing more than the anguished expression of European Christianity in the face of death.

Nothing remains of the ancient cult of the dead but the flowers on the graves, and the wreath on the Tomb of the Unknown Soldier.

What kind of new human beings does Western Christianity wish to generate in Africa? Does the gospel help us to become true to themselves? Can we be at peace with our conscience, if conversion requires that we live separated from the dead of our family, without any possibility of contacting them in the periods of crisis? What new kind of people does God want to construct among us out of our unique African traits? Isn't communion with the ancestors a mark of our culture?

We have seen old sages shun new religions which run counter to their ideal of life, and which disintegrate families and break vital bonds.[24] At the moment when the church is opening itself to the human and spiritual values of non-European civilizations, Africa challenges its own nascent Christianity—far from us to organize a ready-made faith and cult. Rather, let a new language for the gospel come forth from the lives of our people with their deeply rooted belief in the ancestors. Isn't this question of language at the heart of our common faith? Our Christian faith does not intend to express itself through new forms of cultural violence.

Notes

1. John Mbiti has gathered a long list of such expressions from many parts of Africa which are cited in *African Religions and Philosophy* (New York: Doubleday Anchor, 1970), pp. 175-176.

2. Ibid., pp. 175-176.

3. On the role of kinship in Africa, consult D. Paulme, "La notion de parenté dans les sociétés africaines," *Cahiers Internationaux de Sociologie* 15 (1953).

4. Mbiti, *African Religions*, p. 76.

5. Anselme Titianma Sanon, *Tièrce église ma mère ou la conversion d'une communauté païenne au Christ* (Paris: Beauchesne, 1972), p. 246.

6. *Le Siège apostolique et les missions*, Vol. II (Paris: Union Missionnaire du Clergé, 1959), p. 154.

7. The "Instruction" of the Sacred Congregation of Propaganda Fide of 1659 may be found in *Sacrae Congregationis de Propaganda Fide*, I (Rome: 1907), pp. 42-43. The relevant text also appears in *The Chinese Rites Controversy* by George Minamiki (Chicago: Loyola University Press, 1985), pp. 31-32.

8. "Africae Terrarum," Message of Pope Paul VI to the Sacred Hierar-

chy and all the people of Africa for the promotion of the religious, civil, and social welfare of their continent, October 29, 1967. The full text of this document and others of interest are in *Modern Mission Documents and Africa*, edited by Raymond Hickey, O.S.A. (Dublin: Dominican Publications, 1982), pp. 176-197.

9. The death of the victim of the sacrifice will probably raise some questions for the Christian who has read the "Letter to the Hebrews."

10. For details, see J.-F. Vincent, "Divination et possession chez les Mofu montagnards du Nord-Cameroun," *Journal de la Société des Africainistes* 41 (1971): 118 ff.

11. See Meinrad Hebga, *Croyances et guérison* (Yaoundé: CLE, 1973).

12. Vincent, "Divination et possesion chez les Mofu," p. 71.

13. R. Deniel, *Religions dans la ville. Croyances et changements sociaux à Abidjan* (Abidjan: Inades, 1975), pp. 76-77.

14. The *mens* of Propaganda Fide of February 28, 1941 is discussed in Minamiki, *The Chinese Rites Controversy* (Chicago: Loyola University Press, 1985), pp. 201-202. The Latin text is in *Collectanea Commissionis Synodalis* XIV (1941): 562.

15. The French text of this statement of the Bishops of Madagascar of October 17, 1935 appears in *Vingt-cinq ans de pastorale missionnaire*, edited by Joseph Greco (Issy-les Moulineaux: Les Presses Missionnaires, 1958), pp. 202-203.

16. Ch. Ph. Ariès, "La mort inversée. Le changement des attitudes devant la mort dans les sociétés occidentales," *Maison-Dieu* 101 (1970): 57-89.

17. *La Documentation Catholique* 1546 (September 1960): 767-772. The English text, "An African Christianity," is in *Modern Missionary Documents and Africa*, edited by Raymond Hickey (Dublin: Dominican Publications, 1982), pp. 200-208.

18. Here I have particularly in mind "The Constitution of the Sacred Liturgy" (December 4, 1963), no. 37; and "Declaration on the Relations of the Church to Non-Christian Religions" (October 28, 1965). See *Vatican Council II: The Conciliar and Post Conciliar Documents*, edited by Austin Flannery (Northport, NY: Costello, 1975).

19. Trent, 25th session.

20. "Lumen Gentium," no. 16, Flannery, p. 367.

21. "Lumen Gentium," no. 16, Flannery, p. 367.

22. Justin, *First Apology*, Chapter 46.

23. The phrase is from H. Urs von Balthasar, "Le Saint-Esprit, l'Inconnu au-delà du Verbe," *Lumières et Vie* 67 (1964).

24. Sanon, *Tièrce église*, p. 168.

Chapter 3

Telling the Story
of God's Revelation

Many ethnic groups in black Africa embraced the Christian faith after a long and somewhat muffled resistance; Christianity really came into being only after this resistance had been broken. In Africa, in a way, Christianity appears to be a religion of the losers, whose fear and insecurity have become its major traits. Wasn't Christianity's victory over traditional religions perhaps a deadly blow to its credibility? One has to start with this fact to understand why Christianity remains outside the intimate life of the African.

After a century of missionary work, few Africans feel really at home in the church. For most converts, Christianity is the religion of the cities; in the villages, the people practice fetishism.[1] Very often—and this is very revealing—the church makes converts in the bush (the villages), but the city takes away their faith. What is certain is that in many African countries Christians are defined above all as people who had to abandon their traditional customs. In fact, a person exists as a Christian in a "church," which, despite its catechism and sacraments, really amounts to no more than an empty shell or frame with no real influence on social problems. Because the Christianity of missioners supplies no answers to the difficulties of daily life, Christians continue to follow the traditions of their villages or districts. This ambivalence is the source of many tensions that mark the people.

Such situations have consequences, including the proliferation and strong influence of sects among young people confused about the future, and the polite indifference of African intellectuals who view Christianity as an out-of-date religion in a world come of age. These factors should force the church to re-examine its faith and its presence in African society, or else Christianity will be seen as a religion only for women and children. Finally, the search for a faith that speaks to Africans should be aware of the dynamism of traditional religions in responding to the current crises in African society.[2] It is striking to see the resurgence of magical-religious beliefs and practices in regions where the Christian presence seemed solidly established.[3] And finally, the vigor of independent churches, which attempt to interpret Christianity to make it more meaningful and useful, challenge the official churches.[4]

We must listen to the world in which the African lives if we want to move beyond Christianity as it is today—a religion alive only inside churches and a religion usually confined to books, while the majority of the faithful can neither read nor write! It is from this perspective that we must also question and redefine Christian sacramentalism in terms of African cultures. How can we reevaluate the meaning and significance of the Christian mystery, taking into account African symbolism, in a universe where the African searches for concrete happiness within the shadow of the ancestors? How can we celebrate the presence of the Risen One in a land of symbolic forces where the mystery of the African "night" is revealed in a concrete and sensitive way?

A complete and definitive answer to these questions is impossible. However, I will outline some areas for study and reflection within Christian African experience; such reflection is an urgent task for the African church.

Black African Symbolism

It is necessary to emphasize again the importance of symbolism in the socio-cultural context where Africans actually live their lives. Among the many ethnic groups of the grassland and forest, among those who keep cattle and those who farm, symbolism plays a very key role in daily life. Technologically deprived black Africa is overwhelmingly richer in signs and symbols than it is in physical tools. In a universe where all things speak, signs play an important role in every socio-religious practice. In one sense, the African civilization is a civilization of symbols.[5] In it, relationships between one human being and another, and between human beings and nature, pass through the invisible, the symbolic place where all reality acquires meaning. Then the truly real is invisible and the visible is only appearance—all is symbol. Africans live then in a "forest of symbols," a unique way of maintaining their relationships to the universe.[6]

Systematic use of symbols is a dominant feature of most societies without written languages. A symbol, however, is accessible only to "insiders"; thus symbols mark the frontiers of a community and separate people into groups. Full of meaning for some, they are indecipherable for others. This symbolic capital defining each society is revealed in patterns of behavior that distinguish outsiders from insiders. The ways that Africans employ certain postures and use gestures are marks of a culture and a language common to all members of that group. As a result, to deprive Africans of their essential symbols also deprives them of their self-awareness and tears them from the reality that has integrated them into the very system by which, through its symbols, they are striving to overcome the contradiction between life and death.

The symbolic order in Africa concerns the whole drama of existence that expresses the relationships between human beings and the invisible. Any religion is itself a total language, a means of expression allowing people to grasp fully their unity with the entire world, and to communicate with it. In Africa, religion is a system of signs and symbols that attributes primacy to the spoken word.[7] Africa's symbolic system, which can lead to an understanding of the African "language," includes forms of oral expression, gestures, rituals, actions, and so on, embracing institutions, objects and beings.

The kola nut is a good example of this symbolism. In its richness of meaning, the kola nut represents all wisdom. No assembly or wedding can take place without it. In fact, each wedding gift is symbolic: in addition to the kola nut, millet, salt, cowrie shells, tobacco, and the calabash (a type of gourd) are traditionally essential items. The calabash is not simply a woman's utensil; it is also the image of the womb. The Kirdi of northern Cameroon mark a woman's grave with a calabash. It is believed that the whole world once emerged from a calabash whose halves stand for the heavens and the earth.[8] The cosmic dimension of marriage has been clearly explained by Zahan: the man is the sun and the woman the earth.[9] In some tribes this identification of a woman with the earth is shown by the fruits she brings with her when she moves into her husband's house.

Since African culture is overwhelmingly orality, speech between people is heavy with symbolism. Africans express themselves through an infinite variety of symbols drawn from the concrete universe of their experience, wherein language finds its meaning. The spoken word itself contains a system of symbols for reality. For example, among the Ewondo and the Bulu, to "count the nights" means to live as man and wife. Monsignor Sidibe reported that the Bambara use the phrase "the bed" to express sexual intercourse: thus, "The bed came about between this man and this woman."[10]

Within this oral culture, proverbs are an important form of symbolic thought and imagery. Equally important is the story, which mingles the real with the imaginary, and creates archetypal heroes who are both images and symbols.[11] In particular, the animal world of the black African story-teller is an inexhaustible well of symbols pertaining to daily life. The turtle incarnates wisdom, prudence, and skill in the stories of forest peoples. Among the Bambara, the elephant represents the immensity of knowledge; the lion stands for the "educative and noble aspect of training"; and the hyena for "objective knowledge available to human beings."[12]

The story also has an initiatory function, as seen in the story of the hare that always triumphs over the hyena. Here African pedagogy introduces the young to the basic symbolism of life and death. The deep meaning of the characters in the story is related to the drama of the creation of a world that has been disrupted by a rebellious creature and put back in order by ritual activity. These stories illustrate at the same time both the order and disorder of the universe, and the triumph of life over death. Furthermore, their cosmic aspect is augmented by the cathartic function of laughter.

In countless myths, which are a unique way of expressing the primordial situations of human existence, the lizard is the messenger of death, and the chameleon, of resurrection.[13] The Bamileke use the toad as God's agent to announce death to human beings.[14] Among the coastal peoples of Cameroon, the crocodile is linked to a mythology of water spirits, and the Beti tell the story of crossing the Yom River on the back of an enormous serpent.

Symbolism based on snakes is widespread in the myths of African kingdoms. Among the Bamoun in Cameroon, a snake watches over the entrance to the city of Foumban because it is the symbol of the people and of royalty, summarizing both their history and wisdom. The snake reappears in Benin, in Nigeria, and among the Ngbandi of the Ubangi, where it symbolizes royal strength. Throughout forest regions, the owl is associated with sorcery and bad luck. Among the people of Cameroon, the trap-door spider is able to read the future; among the Akan and Ashanti, it stands for wisdom.[15]

A special feature of African linguistic usage is its parsimony—one word serves several ends. Naming a child conveys a program of life and a message; it is also a technique, an action, a rite of protection and of defense.[16] Intentionally ugly names are sought for children to shelter them from hostile spirits. Thus the African system of personal names is a sort of symbolic disguise to elude death, steering it away from a child by using a horrible or contemptible name. The Kirdi of northern Cameroon who follow this practice give many of their children intentionally comic names. Thus the symbolism of name-giving integrates language into daily life.

Symbolism of the Physical World

The inanimate world is also a source of symbolism of astounding wealth. Thus fire stands for the process of death and resurrection. This ambivalence is found again in the person of the blacksmith, the man of death who conducts burials among the Mafa and Kapsiki of the north. But among agricultural groups, the blacksmith, the master of fire, who rips metal from the earth and turns it into hoes, is the civilizing hero. A chain leads from the primordial fire stolen by the blacksmith to the granary where the fruits of the earth are stored. Dogon thought sums up this emotional and logical continuity with astonishing brevity—they use the word "stolen" for the granary.[17] Without the fire and without the iron of the hoe, there would be no harvest to store.

Elsewhere fire represents the source of fecundity or sometimes symbolizes strength and wealth. Among the Fali, fire, often linked with the sun, is associated with edible grain. The Zulgo, another mountain people of the north, have a festival of fire at the time of the ripening of the millet. For the Dogon, fire is "the warmth of the word."[18]

The symbolism of water appears in rituals of blessing, marriage, healing, and purification. Among the traditional Bantu, even saliva is important; spitting in the face of another is not an insult, but a rite of blessing. Similarly, there can be no speech among the Dogon without saliva; the primacy attributed to the spoken word springs from its close kinship to life and fecundity, "since the first word was a damp word."[19] The Kirdi sprinkle water on newlyweds to bless them. The Beti throw "evil" into the running water of a river to be carried far away. The stream is a receptacle of cosmic forces and therefore a preferred location for certain rituals. Among the Ewondo, crossing a mythical river is a symbolic test where a judgment is made about their access to the Beyond. A basic element like fire and oil, water is responsible for germination and assures the formation of all new life. The skin of a drum is moistened with water to stretch it, but also because the water carries the word of the Monitor and of the ancestors who control the lives of human beings.

The symbolism of vegetation in black Africa centers on trees, which speak the language of life and death.[20] The Bamileke have a tree of peace. The Bassa believe that in the beginning life sprang forth from a tree; just by walking around it, one can recover youth. But this tree was uprooted by God at the time of the primordial separation. Among the Kirdi the stalk and grain of millet have a sexual symbolism.[21] For the Dogon the seed is female, and passes through a physiological cycle known as the "menses of the millet."

Like the techniques of the smithy, pottery is full of symbolism. Even musical instruments, such as the rattle, the harp, the androgynous drums, and the balaphon of the Beti, all symbolize the primordial duality of the world. The idea of symbolic fecundity is absorbed in an overall concept of music, which is considered to be essentially fecund.[22]

Space in relation to humans is also important. Throughout Africa the four cardinal points of the compass enter into the play of symbols in daily life.[23] Men and women sleep in directions appro-

Telling the Story of God's Revelation   **39**

priate for each, and are also buried in that way.[24] But the specific symbolism of directions is linked to the particular set of values in each society; the Beti of the south, for example, turn their dead towards the west where God withdrew after the drama of the primordial separation.

The symbolic opposition of right and left corresponds generally to the two sexes. In central Africa, a man calls his left arm "my female arm" and a woman calls her right arm "my male arm"; left is always female and right, male. In the Central African Republic, the same words are actually used for both concepts. Among the Bamileke the right side stands for royal strength and power—the chief always takes his place on the right; the hunter strikes his quarry with his right hand; but the spoils of war are put on the left—the side of the defeated. The left is also the side of safety and tenderness; the woman is always at the left of a man.[25] The Ewondo would never invite a friend to sit down on their left side but always on their right, to indicate their intimacy. The Bamileke interpret omens in terms of right and left. If a red bird crosses one's path from right to left, it is a bad sign; from left to right, a good sign. The Kirdi work out techniques of divination in the same way; a chicken that falls to the left, for example, is a sign of bad luck.

Likewise the symbolism of numbers is important, although the meaning varies from one society to another. Among the Kirdi, odd numbers are masculine and even, feminine. This symbolism plays a big role in ceremonies for births and funerals. An infant is presented to the sun after a certain number of days determined by its sex. The end of the mourning period is established in the same way.

The Bamileke have two sacred numbers: "8" marks fullness (a week there has eight days); "9" stands for power in the council of a chief. Thus a decision pronounced by the nine councillors of a chief is binding. For the Bassa, man is "5" in so far as one considers sexual parts in the definition of a human being. The Kirdi drink twice from the same calabash as a token of friendship, since a man has two testicles. Among the Bassa and the Beti of the south, "9" stands for perfection and totality. The Beti tradition says that God has given people nine duties. Among the Bassa, sentencing a person to walk nine times around a sacred tree excludes that person from the world of the living and hands over the person to the ancestors.

As numbers and location symbolize the difference between male and female and left and right, so colors stand for life and death. I will not describe this symbolism as it has been worked out in detail by Engelbert Mveng.[26]

It is important to keep in mind that the concepts of male and female are expressed through a great variety of symbols; male and female—which oppose and yet complement each other—sum up the entire creation, which is characterized by this great duality. The sexuality of humans seems to be projected throughout the entire universe. Thus, the whole world is sexually divided and mirrors on humanity its own image, at once male and female.

If we view the world as a book whose meaning must be read and decoded, we must always remember to interpret the signs around us in terms of our own humanity. Everything is part of this relationship of signifier and signified, beginning with human beings who are a microcosm of the world. Man is symbolized by the sun and by the right; woman by the earth and the moon, and by the left. Inversely, the world is also endowed with sexuality: "the sky is male because it covers the earth, a masculine function; the earth is receptive, and hence feminine and maternal."[27] In one of the most typical characteristics of African symbolism, humanity thus encapsulates the whole universe. Placed in a global context where human beings realize that life has no meaning without death, African symbols can describe the situation of humans in the world. As the victory of the hare over the hyena reveals, death does not have the last word; African symbolism dramatizes the victory of life over death.

Symbolism in the Initiation Ritual

Initiation into adulthood in black Africa represents precisely this contest between life and death and, in the end, the triumph of life. But we must note that symbolic language is a goal, since its use is forbidden to the uninitiated. The Bambara learn certain basic signs at the time of their initiation.[28] Initiation is not only a decisive experience bringing about a new state of being, a mode of existence in the world with reference to the ancestors; it is also a true language in itself, which is composed of gestures and words. It concentrates an organic totality of symbolic demeanor and actions that are emotionally charged and pregnant with meaning.

The seclusion of the initiants in an enclosure or a special camp removed from their village represents the shrinking of their universe. This seclusion is to help them re-experience their life in the womb. This marginal period of time is necessary before gaining the status of an authentic adult person. Through a ritualized sequence of instructions and ordeals, it expresses the slowness of passage though life. In this manner, initiation implies both a symbolic dying, corresponding to the phase of marginalization, and a rebirth. In many African societies initiation is held in a place where one is said "to die," and the seclusion in the bush is called a "burial."

Circumcision, a part of the initiation ritual, is itself a reminder of death. Mothers "lament" the disappearance of their child. Towards the end of the initiant's seclusion, everything connected with this "putting to death" is destroyed. Then the initiant receives a new name and leaves the compound with a fist raised in victory, and a body painted with red kaolin powder, the color of life. Initiation sums up both the rituals of birth and burial, repeating the drama of life and death. To undergo initiation is to die and to be reborn. At the moment, then, when the initiant passes from nature (the forest) to culture (the village), the youth receives the secrets of the ethnic group and becomes ready to have children. At the very same time, the youth relives the great myths of the creation of humanity and the world. The time of initiation allows African youth to relive the genesis of the universe and experience the gestation of the world—everything that happened in the beginning happens again in this ritual whereby humanity participates in the drama of the victory of life over death.[29]

Reawakening the Wellsprings of Existence

If Christianity wants to reach Africans, to speak to their hearts, and to enter their consciousness and the space where their soul breathes, it must change. To do so, Christianity must do violence to itself and break the chains of Western rationality, which means almost nothing in the African civilization of the symbol. Without some form of epistemological break with the Scholastic universe, Christianity has little chance of reaching the African. Catholicism has made the language of Aristotle its official theological language.

Yet Jesus of Nazareth, whose manner of speech echoed that of peasants and shepherds, did not use it; neither do Blacks in Africa. Christianity in Africa has played this theological game and been transformed into a kind of iconoclasm that has led to the perversion of symbols into simple allegories. The whole Scholastic and academic pedagogy of the West penalizes symbolism and ridicules symbolic thought.[30] The collision of the gospel with the African world compels the church to restore to symbols their place and value in the encounter of humanity with God. After all, that encounter takes place through Christ who is the primordial sacrament—the manifestation of the Invisible One in the visible, the irruption of God into the perceived world, the domain of all that can be felt, heard, or touched (I John 1:1-3).

The real scandal of our faith is the intervention of God in the web of human history (John 1:14). If we are to become contemporaries of Jesus Christ, we must overcome the distance—both historical and cultural—that separates us from the gospel. This will not happen unless we move beyond the Scholastic categories of the catechism and translate our message about Jesus of Nazareth into the language of African culture, the language of symbols. Such an endeavor requires a kind of "ethics of transgression," by which we dare to break away from foreign categories of thought, foreign institutions, and foreign acts of faith, all heavy with the weight of the Greco-Latin West. It will allow us, in the end, to rediscover the superabundance of meaning in the Christian mystery that lies within our own cultural context. We must deliver Christianity in Africa from its captivity to the Scholastic and conceptual traditions of Western dogmatism.

In the words of the French savant Bachelard, we need to "reawaken the wellsprings" to rediscover the path that will free humanity, currently suffocating within narrow rationalism, for openness and participation. If we are to live our faith in a context marked by the basic symbolism of life and death, we must find our way back to the pool of Siloam (John 9:7) where, like the blind man who washed his eyes and had his sight restored, we can once again claim our primordial language. "Symbolic language is not an historical avatar or a cultural accident of revelation; rather, faith can be expressed only symbolically, and every other type of discourse must be subordinated to this symbolic expression."[31] God communicates with humanity under the veil of symbols; words, gestures, and signs must all work together to manifest God. Because the essence of the Christian mystery is ineffable, it can be spoken of only in veiled words, in images and symbols.

The celebration of this mystery arises from poetry or, better yet, from art. Indeed, basic symbols reveal God more concretely than clear and distinct ideas; the atmosphere of celebration arises more from *poesis* than from *ratio*. Christianity cannot dispense with the symbolic language that scholasticism eliminated from Christian theology. In fact the first Christians and the Fathers of the Church did not disdain the use of symbols to express their faith and make it intelligible to others.[32] Today we need to reactualize the Christian mystery within a cultural structure, where "symbolism expresses the destiny of humanity everywhere as a struggle between life and death."[33] Both the gospel and Africa require that of us.

We must not forget that the Christian mystery is the mystery of the Cross. Hence, the plant kingdom penetrates the heart of the gospel message. The Preface to the Triumph of the Cross says that "we should be saved through the wood of the cross. The tree of our defeat became our tree of victory; where life was lost, there life has been restored."

The dimensions of such a mystery are shown in the four cardinal directions commonly used by the African to discover the basic and familiar symbolism of the totality. The cross-like motif enables the African to grasp the cosmic dimension of salvation by the Tree of the Cross, whose life-giving virtue is described in the New Testament in the perspective of the new creation: "In the middle of the street of the city, on one side of the river and on the other, is the tree of life bearing twelve fruits, one each month; and whose leaves can heal the nations" (Rev. 22:2-3). Because Jesus contains in himself the whole work of God—creation and redemption, time and history—we cannot attain God by lifting ourselves out of the world, or by isolating ourselves from time and space; we cannot attain God in the pure transcendance of the spirit, or in the absolute. No. We find God concretely at the human level, there where we are most deeply ourselves. In our flesh all is united—tree and animal, water and wine, light and fire, word and bread—all assumed together by the incarnate Word. For if salvation takes on flesh, every act of God crucified penetrates the most physical

aspects of incarnate existence. This is how we must view the sacramental meaning of the church as it was restored by Vatican II.[34]

The time of salvation is the time of the signs through which the
mystery of faith is realized. The risen Christ, in the austerity of his
absence from our senses, and the *kenosis* (Phil. 2:7) of his glory,
becomes our contemporary in a type of *Parousia*, or second
coming, by means of the sacraments. Each sacrament incorporates one aspect of the remembrance of the Lord. We must retell
and celebrate his coming, using the basic symbols of our relationship to the world. We must proclaim this reality of salvation,
remembering that Christianity transmits and actualizes an
event—not just a word—that should be continually renewed
through the sharing of bread and wine. The Word of God is
identifed with the event of the risen Christ.

In Africa, the confrontation between the message of the gospel
and the African universe must bring forth a meaning with the
power to transform the lives of African Christians. Today the faith
of the church in Africa is in danger of death because the church
tends to forget that its cultural dimensions are marked by its Greco-
Latin heritage. If the faith of Africans is not to die, it must become
a vision of the world that they can feel is theirs; European cultural
orientations must be stripped away. There is an urgent need to
reject present foreign models of expression if we are to breathe new
life into the spoken Word. Our church must experience a Passover
of language, or the meaning of the Christian message will not be
understood.

One of the primary tasks of Christian reflection in black Africa
is to totally reformulate our basic faith through the mediation of
African culture. In place of the cultural presuppositions of Western
Christianity, namely *logos* and *ratio*, we must now substitute the
logic of African symbolism. Beginning with the ecclesial furrow
where the language of faith germinates, we must restore the gospel's power to speak to Africans through the primordial symbols of
their existence.

Toward a Living Relationship between Humanity and God

Our first task is to rediscover the meaning of the mystery of God
that is characteristic of rural African villages. We have to tell of the

Christian mystery in a universe where God exists beyond language, where God cannot be named by human beings. In African society, an exceptional awareness of divine transcendence is present; for, in spite of their acute sense of the power of the spoken word and the significance of any act of naming, Africans refuse to call God by name.[35]

In black Africa God remains beyond the control of humanity and words—so distant that God is seen as the Chief of the Obscure or the Master of the Forgotten Ones, a term used by the Guiziga of the north.[36] In that realm of God where analogy is the principle of rational discourse, symbolic discourse appeals to metaphor. God surges up from symbolic discourse as an absent subject whom we can neither grasp nor appropriate, but only evoke. Because Africans are accustomed to seeing things with eyes that move from sign to meaning and from the visible to the invisible, it is possible for us Africans to develop a new symbolic understanding of our relationship with God. Christ brings a radical newness to this relationship that we call conversion. This symbolism makes the converted African into a theologian-poet who transforms the universe by giving it a new sphere of representation.

In order to evangelize black Africa, we must establish a relationship with the "living revelation" where God begins to speak through an apostle of a base community, using an African style to speak to Africans. The pedagogy of faith must develop a method of integrating the narrative of the Passion and Resurrection of Jesus into the memory of our people. The art of the black African storyteller can be of service. We must talk about God in lands where the millet granary is the very image of the world and says far more to people than the vine or the wheat field. We dream of a church where God speaks to these people with images and symbols rooted in the hard soil of the grassland and the trees of the forest.

Africa is a setting where human beings search for communion with God. The drama of the primordial break between God and the world is deeply imprinted on the religious consciousness of Bantu and Sudanese Africa.[37] In such a context, it makes more sense to talk of our faith in the good news of God's presence in the world through Christ using the very techniques of African oral tradition. It is meaningless to make Christianity a religion of the written word in a civilization of the spoken word! The West encloses the

Christian faith in its system of writing; hence missionaries have made Christian Africans into "children who read." Today young Africans have access to printed materials; however, when caught off guard while reading to themselves, they are usually reading out loud. Silent reading is a Western tradition. Even educated Africans liberate the spoken word in the end, because they really understand the text only by the sounds that constitute it. The written characters seen by the eye determine sound, which, in turn, conveys meaning. This commonplace experience of understanding by hearing demands that the African church forget its obsession with the written word—whether the Bible or the catechism—and relocate the Christian message in the world of spoken language. To "tell God's story" to people who can't read or write, we must proclaim orally the message of Easter. We must replace the silent reading of the text with what Jousse calls "manducation of the Word."

Experience in our local communities shows that a true celebration of the Word can happen only in the context of gospel "palaver." This is far more than just a reading of sacred texts: it is a festival of language shared by the whole community, which involves grasping the Word, searching for its meaning, questions and answers, prayers and chants. Gesture is also a part of this celebration because Africans do not speak with images and symbols alone, but with their whole body, with mimicry and body language. In a true liturgy of the Word, the whole community sets about discovering the meaning of God's message, perhaps for a particular place or a specific group of people. The liturgy includes the acclamations of the assembly and its agreement or disagreement, which are punctuated with unanimous shouts. Everyone's voice is heard and the rhythm of everyone's feet is felt. Nothing is planned in advance. The gifts of improvisation and creativity triumph, in the style of a village gathering where some event in community life requires collective decision-making.

In black Africa, why can't the church rediscover this incantatory power of the Word, shouted or rhythmically recited, of dance and chant, and of the language of the drum? After all, the message itself is temporal. The church should learn from the old masters of the spoken word who have been teaching Africans for millennia. Their mode of expression is always accompanied by the judicious use of gestures, by the rhythm of the body, now factual, now emotional or imitative and, as a whole, inseparable from a rhythmic and creative use of repetition to aid in memorization.

The churches of Africa dream of a proclamation of the Easter mystery that would recall the declamatory style of the griot or of the player of the *mvet*, whereby we could rediscover all the riches of the oral tradition. The liturgy would gather up all the techniques of the Word and all the virtues of silence; it would involve the participation of the body and attain cosmic dimensions. In this way, the liturgy of the Word would authentically recite sacred history. The art of telling the story of God's revelation to humanity would produce a drama lived through once again with meaning for each moment, for each cycle of time. Christ's victory over death would be the guiding thread of the cycle of the liturgical year, through the "unrolling of day and night," since all of lived time is re-experienced in the symbolic rhythm of the resurrection.

Toward an African Liturgy

By its very being, the Christian mystery is gesture and sacrament. Ever since God fashioned a body for his Son (Heb. 10:5), the communication of human beings with God has taken place on the level of symbols. The universe of signs is the realm where, through faith, we can touch the body of the Risen One. In that universe, through gestures rooted in the great acts of God throughout history, Christ reaches us in person, symbolically, through the action of the Holy Spirit.

The Second Vatican Council proclaimed that the work of salvation accomplished by Christ is realized in the liturgy of the church.[38] The work of our redemption becomes real in every liturgical celebration of the mysteries of the faith where the church is again the gathered community and where the force of the Word of God makes it the Body of Christ. In this way, liturgical acts bring us the mystery of the presence and the action of Christ by using the basic signs of Christianity. Can the African church participate in this mystery by limiting itself to ready-made texts and prayers translated into the vernacular, with the possibility of adding indigenous musical instruments?

Perhaps we will no longer celebrate the liturgy of the four European seasons of winter, spring, summer, and fall. Such a liturgy has no meaning in the tropics, where people organize their lives around the dry season and the rainy season. This is particularly true of the grasslands of the Sahel. Similarly, why is there so little interest in designing African liturgical vestments in a culture that could restore to Christianity this rich symbolism of forms and colors—especially when these symbols are missing in the cultural context of the West? The old rites used a variety of colors, which were linked to the liturgical seasons and the nature of the religious festivals. Over the course of time the liturgical colors for the dead have changed from black to violet—a violet that drifts frequently into light pink, as if to brighten up the celebration of Christian death. On ordinary Sundays the priest wears green. Some colors used in the liturgy have a universal meaning, but such is not the case with white and black. Why can't the symbolism of colors in the Christian liturgy be inspired directly by nature, and by the location of the church? This is not an unimportant question, because it is not evident to all people, for example, that Africans find no meaning in the violet vestments worn by the celebrant of a Eucharist. Why use white garments for the newly baptized in a culture where white is the color of the dead? In black Africa, red is the color of life and of the victory of life over death; red alone can symbolize the participation of the baptized in the glory of the Risen One.

Again, does pouring water over the head of the baptized adequately express the mystery of the death and resurrection of Christ in which we participate through baptism? Doesn't immersion in running water have more meaning? Likewise, has anyone reflected on the importance of Christian names, taking into consideration the importance of the African symbolism of names, and the biblical tradition wherein people carry a name corresponding to their assigned role? How can we use traditional African names and give them a Christian meaning?

The great theme of African sacred history is that, since after the withdrawal of God, human beings still feel a nostalgia for communion with the divinity. But does the Eucharist as it is celebrated in our African communities adequately make use of the basic theme of a meal—an event at which human beings are graciously given food that lets them live in nearness to God? The question is raised because African cultural traditions have developed an authentic symbolism of the meal.[39] The church has correctly insisted on the sacrificial character of the Mass. However the changes that have occurred throughout the history of Christian worship demonstrate that the church has settled on normative elements for the Eucharist, which fail to convey the great richness of this mystery to all ways of thinking and all peoples. Today we encounter the Risen One in a liturgical action where the breaking of bread and the sharing of wine do not form part of an actual meal. For a long time the symbolism of a true meal has been abandoned for communion with bread alone. In black Africa, we ask God for food in the Lord's Prayer—the fruit of our land and of our culture; but at the Lord's Table, we use a food that is the fruit of another land and another culture.

Our difficulty in translating the names of the imported Eucharistic elements into our local languages is a measure of the foreignness of the Eucharistic liturgy in our African communities. We are always struck by the lack of symbols of the Eucharist. Monsignor Anselme Sanon has affirmed with rare courage:

> Deny it as we will, the Eucharist is an artificial meal, prefabricated and not the fruit of our culture. We observe this often at the time of the Offertory, when the congregation brings its offerings. When the offerings are concrete and truly come from the people, the Offertory is an interlude in the rite. But if there is no ceremony of offerings coming from the people, the meal and the sacrifice are prefabricated.[40]

Instead of reproducing a style of celebration marked by a foreign culture, our Christian communities should strive to create, in the Spirit, our own way of manifesting the One who has the power to free us through the gift of his Body.

How then can we express this presence in the Eucharist, so that the hearing of the Word, the offering, and the sharing of communion will all be authentic symbols of the meal? It is not just the bread or the wine, but the whole meal that symbolizes communion with the Christ who offers himself in sacrifice. If we lose the totality of the basic symbolism of the meal through which Christian initiation is consummated, then the meaning of the Lord's Supper crumbles, and with it the participation of those present by their acts and communion. This is a central problem. Christianity rests on an original symbolism in two parts—immersion in the waters of baptism and the breaking of bread. The way we translate these two actions into African symbolism is the most obvious test of the catholicity, or lack thereof, of the church. Admitting that the field of millet or sorghum is growing to the glory of God, when will these humble fruits of the African soil become part of the Eucharist? A translation of the faith is not enough; the church must transmit the same faith through different signs.

Certainly these rites should not be turned into a new fetishism. If the Eucharist, the "summit and source of all evangelization," were to be affirmed as the only means to receive salvation, it would still not answer the many questions raised by the faith in an African context. The insistence of the church on the Mass can be understood in the particular context of the Counter-Reformation. No one denies the importance of the Mass. May we simply suggest that the Mass not be an absolute? In Christianity, Light is strictly inseparable from the Word, of which Light is one particular aspect. We must enhance this union between the Word and the Life in black Africa where the spoken word is so efficacious.

A Faith for the Whole Person

In our African societies, dreams are the language of the Beyond through the imagination, and Night is the time, above all, when the mysterious forces of the universe come alive. In such a world, how can we live our relationship with Christ, ignoring that the dead speak to the living through dreams? Sickness itself is an illustration. In black Africa, sickness is not experienced as an objective fact, but as a negative value, a scandal that belongs in the anthropological realm of evil and misfortune. It is not felt as a phenomenon that comes to strike a particular individual, but rather as a disturbance of social relationships. Thus sickness is the business of the entire family—indeed, of the whole village.

It makes sense that the techniques of healing cannot be separated from the symbolic universe from which they emerge. Sickness is inextricably involved in the relationship of human beings with each other and with the universe. The evil that one sees does not provide any information about the deep reality symbolized by the sickness.

Thus the African universe of sickness is inseparable from the universe of spirits, which appears like a logical language that accounts for the order and disorder of the world, misfortune, failure and death. In this state of insecurity where Africans are helpless and ready to resort to any means to resolve their dilemmas, and where sorcery and traditional medicine are flourishing, the church cannot ignore the problems experienced by people facing adversity. The African church needs a deeper understanding of sacraments that is more meaningful than that authorized by the liturgical reform in Rome. It must search for a better way to celebrate the different stages of Christian initiation, marriage, and burial.

The church must not avoid the existential questions of those who live in communication with the ancestors. The phenomena of witchcraft and possession are signs of a time of crisis when Africans feel a need for security. Faced with occult forces and influences, they frantically search for symbolic objects and for a whole way of life that will protect them against sorcery. It is of vital importance to provide an answer to these questions of life and death for which Africans today go out and look for marabouts, diviners, and healers. Answering these questions is as important as resolving the scruples of missionaries, or puzzling over whether a polygamous village elder can receive the sacraments. In a period of social upheaval and disintegration, we must encounter Africans in their dreams and anguish, and pay most serious attention to the realm of the imaginary.

The question then of an African symbolism to express the Christian message is the demand of a faith that is open to the concrete realities of people and their world. An adequate response to this vital question could turn the church into a true sign of hope for those who live in despair. But in Africa this endeavor takes place in the midst of a confrontation of culture, and in a context where the powerlessness of the official churches to reveal the liberating power of the gospel has allowed the appearance of black Messianisms, symptoms of a certain hope in the midst of misery, sickness, and oppression, and the incarnation of the dynamism of revelation in the history of today's Africa.

In order to rethink the Christian message in light of the actual demands of black Africa, we must free the gospel from a Christianity that has become too middle class. The challenge facing the church is to live out the faith, not only around sacramental rites in places of worship, but starting with the struggles and hopes for human liberation. The faith must be lived in the cultural settings of African society. Today, only the "prophetic churches" are interested in a prophetic witness to the Word or in the application of the saving power of the Cross to spiritual illnesses. It is urgent, therefore, to consider the problems of exorcism and mental illness as they exist today in Africa. When we confront the actuality of spirit-possession, we have to remember that in the eyes of his contemporaries, Christ was, first of all, a man with power over the spirits. This, more than anything else, is what struck the Apostles (Acts 10:38). Today's pastoral situation in Africa, where the faith comes face to face with the mystery of the Night, and Africans are in relationship with the invisible on every level of their existence—this is where we must find an African expression of the Word of God that will be truly committed to the course of our human history.

Notes

1. R. Deniel, "Religion et changements sociaux," *Recherches de Sciences Religieuses* 63 (1975); and *Religions dans la ville: Croyances et changements sociaux à Abidjan* (Abidjan: INADES, 1975).

2. *Colloque sur les religions africaines, Abidjan, April 1961* (Paris: Présence Africaine, 1962); *Les religions africaines comme sources de valeurs de civilisation, Colloque, Cotonou* (Paris: Présence Africaine, 1972). See also L. V. Thomas and R. Luneau, *La terre africaine et ses religions* (Paris: Larousse, 1974).

3. R. Bureau, "Sorcellerie et prophétisme en Afrique noire," *Études* (April 1967): 467-481.

4. Thomas and Luneau, *La terre africaine*, pp. 322-323.

5. R. Bastide, "Religions africaines et structures de civilisation," *Présence Africaine* 66 (1968): 101.

6. M. Griaule, "Réflexions sur les symboles soudanais," *C.I.S.* XII (1952): 9.

7. G. Calame-Griaule, *Ethnologie et language, la parole chez les Dogon* (Paris: Gallimard, 1965).

8. For more on the cosmic and feminine meaning of the calabash, see M. Griaule, *Dieu d'eau* (Paris: Fayard, 1966).

9. D. Zahan, *La dialectique du verbe chez les Bambara* (Paris and the

Hague: Mouton, 1963), p. 95; A. Hampaté Ba, *Aspects de la civilisation africaine* (Paris: Présence Africaine, 1972).

10. Msgr. Sidibe, "Racines et conditions des communautés africaines," Address at the Synod of 1977; see also CALAO, no. 41-42 (1978): 15.

11. L. S. Senghor, "Préface" to Amadou Koumba, *Les nouveaux contes*; A. Hampaté Ba, *Aspects de la civilisation africaine*, pp. 38-44.

12. L. V. Thomas and R. Luneau, *Les sages dépossédés* (Paris: Larousse, 1977), p. 284, note 104.

13. See E. Mveng, *L'art d'Afrique noire, liturgie cosmique et langage religieux* (Yaoundé, Cameroon: CLE), pp. 149-150; J. Mbiti, *Religions et philosophie africaines* (Yaoundé, Cameroon: CLE, 1972) pp. 149-150; in English, *African Religions and Philosophy* (New York: Praeger, 1969 and London: Heinemann, 1969).

14. Sop Nkamkang Martin, *Contes et légendes du Bamileke*, Vol. 1 (Yaoundé, 1970).

15. J. Mbiti, *Religions et philosophie africaines*, p. 61.

16. M. Houis, *Les noms individuels chez les Mossi* (Dakar: IFAN, 1963); J. Hallaire, "Note sur les noms Sara (Tchad)," *Afrique et Parole* 33-34 (July 1971).

17. M. Griaule, *Réflexions sur les symboles soudanais,* p. 38.

18. Ibid.

19. Ibid.

20. V. Paques, *L'arbre cosmique dans la pensée populaire et dans la vie quotidienne de l'ouest africain* (Paris: Institut d'Ethnologie, 1964); G. Calame-Griaule, "L'arbre au trésor," in *Le thème de l'arbre dans les contes africains*, Bibliothèque de la SELAF, 16 (1969); G. Dieterlen, "Classification des végétaux chez les Dogon," *Journal Africain* 22 (1953).

21. Y. Schaller, *Les Kirdi du Nord-Cameroun* (Strasbourg: Imp. des Dernières Nouvelles, 1973), p. 42.

22. G. Calame-Griaule, *Introduction à l'étude de la musique africaine* (Paris: Richard-Masse, 1957).

23. Thomas and Luneau, *Les sages dépossédés*, p. 118.

24. M. Griaule, "Réflexions sur les symboles soudanais," pp. 90-91.

25. Oral communication from a young priest of the Bamileke, Marcellin Moukam.

26. E. Mveng, *L'art d'Afrique noire*, pp. 31-34; Thomas and Luneau, *Les sages dépossédés*, p. 120; J. Mbiti, *Religions et philosophie africaines*, p. 129.

27. A. Hampaté Ba., *Aspects de la civilisation africaine*, p. 128.

28. G. Dieterlen and Y. Cisse, *Les fondements de la société d'initiation du Komo* (Paris: Mouton, 1972).

29. Mircea Eliade, *Myths, Dreams, and Mysteries: The Encounter*

between Contemporary Faiths and Archaic Realities, trans. Philip Mairet (New York: Harper and Brothers, 1960); Thomas and Luneau, *Les sages dépossédés*, pp. 213-238.

30. G. Durand, "Le statut du symbole et de l'imaginaire aujourd'hui," *Lumière et Vie* 81 (Jan.-March 1967): 42-46.

31. J. P. Magnine, *Pour une poétique de la foi: essai sur le mystère symbolique* (Paris: Cerf, 1969), p. 15.

32. J. Daniélou, *Les symboles chrétiens primitifs* (Paris: du Seuil, 1961), English edition translated by Donald Attwater, *Primitive Christian Symbols* (London: Burns & Oates, 1964); "Le symbolisme des rites baptismaux," *Dieu Vivant* no. 1; L. Bernaert, "Symbolisme mythique de l'eau du baptême," *Maison-Dieu* 22: 94-120.

33. E. Mveng, *L'art d'Afrique noire*, p. 75.

34. "Lumen Gentium," 48; "Gaudium et Spes," 42; "Ad Gentes," 5 in *Vatican Council II: The Conciliar and Post Conciliar Documents*, edited by Austin Flannery (Northport, NY: Costello, 1975).

35. "La nomination de Dieu," *Afrique et Parole* 33-34 (July 1971).

36. R. Jauen, "Le mythe de la retraite de De Bumbulvum chez les Guiziga du Nord-Cameroun," *Afrique et Parole*, 33-34 (July 1971).

37. E. Mveng, *L'art d'Afrique noire*, p. 149; Thomas and Luneau, *Les sages dépossédés*, pp. 135-148.

38. "Constitution on the Sacred Liturgy," 6 in *Vatican Council II*, edited by Flannery.

39. L. V. Thomas, "Essai sur les conduites négro-africaines du repas," *IFAN* (Dakar) VII, B, 162 (1965): 574-635; *Les sages dépossédés*, pp. 51-61.

40. A. T. Sanon, "Où est l'Église universelle?" *Lumière et Vie* 137 (1978): 81.

Chapter 4

The Future of Local Communities

The search for faith and experiences of faith must find its roots in local communities. But how can these communities flourish if they have to look to the outside for all their resources? If everything is given to them by others, how can the men and women who gather around the gospel in Africa express their faith and make use of their own faculties?

Any question related to ministries cannot be separated from reflection on the life of the people of God. A thorough theological investigation of the results of exegesis and history must refer to the church as the place where Christians ask questions and where people hear the Word of God in the reality of the world and history. Any living theology must consider the most important concerns and valid requests coming from communities of faith. From this point of view, I wish to look at the question of ministries in the light of the current problems of African churches.

The renewal of the theology of ministries brought about by Vatican II shows the need to rediscover the Holy Spirit as the key to solving that theological problem. Careful study of the Acts of the Apostles shows that there is *no* ministry except in the Spirit.

Ending the Tyranny of the Clergy

When the Council restored the theology of charisms, it set limits on the theology of ministry that had been dominated until then by legal presuppositions centralizing power in the clergy; by setting these limits, the Council questioned the monolithic structure of the clergy and recognized a diversity of ministries that was more consistent with the apostolic tradition. Vatican II emphasizes this need for a pluralism of ministries:

> Various types of ministry are necessary for the implanting and growth of the Christian community, and once these forms of service have been called forth from the body of the faithful, by the divine call, they are to be carefully fostered and nurtured by all. Among these functions are those of priests, deacons and catechists, and also that of Catholic action. Men and women religious, likewise, play an indispensable role in planting and strengthening the kingdom of Christ in souls, and in the work of further extending it, both by their prayers and active work.[1]

The relevance of this text today is obvious. It implies a new look at ministry based on a new understanding of the relationship between the Spirit and the church. The recognition of different ministries acknowledges the basic truth that ministry is, above all, a common responsibility of the whole church; the ministry of the faithful actualizes the ministry of Christ in the Spirit. The affirmation of the diversity of ministries is a sign that the Spirit always continues working in different ways to inspire the faithful to want to serve the church in different areas. The Spirit is seen at work as the source of this diversity of ministries. It is the Spirit who "shares his gifts as he wills for the common good."[2]

To recognize that the church needs different kinds of ministries is to admit that there is a need to end what has come to be seen as a "tyranny of the clergy." Although Vatican II tackled contemporary problems of the ministry and the life of priests, it did not center its efforts for renewal in that area. The statements of the Council on charisms clearly show that it did not really face the present difficulties of apostolic leadership in Christian communities. The text cited above, with its sampling of the various ministries, places priests, deacons, catechists and Catholic action groups side by side; all these different services of the church, along with those of men and women religious, are to be considered authentic ministries.

In fact, the work of the Council that studied the theology of the laity collided with the church's practice of the unique ministry of priests. Vatican II found that the clergy were not only insufficient in themselves, but were, by themselves alone, incapable of responding to the new needs of the church. To conform to the teachings of Vatican II, the church must restore the importance of the Council's Decree on the Apostolate of the Lay People. It seems impossible today to discuss the ministries within the church without a theology of the laity. The rediscovery of the laity reminds us that there is more to Christian ministry than its present institutional form. The laity must be included in any renewed reflection on ministry. Lay people have their own share of responsibility in the apostolic functions of the whole church. In the words of the Council, "All lay people, through the gifts given them, are at once the witnesses and the living instruments of the mission of the Church itself."[3] Specifically, "Christ fulfills this prophetic office not only by the hierarchy . . . but also by the laity."[4] And finally, "The apostolate of the laity is a sharing in the salvific mission of the Church. Through Baptism and Confirmation all are appointed to this apostolate by the Lord himself."[5]

The Council has clearly gone beyond the old theology of the lay apostolate, which supposedly led to a delegation of hierarchical ministry based, above all, on the new life received through baptism. It also rejected the concept of a "mandate" given to the laity by the episcopate, and acknowledged the specific nature of the ministry of lay persons. Their ministries are not just extensions of the hierarchical ministry, and there is thus no need for them to be recognized through a form of priestly or episcopal ordination. Although consecrating the ministry of lay people in the community does provide a good opportunity for liturgical events,[6] we should eliminate any possibility of clericalizing these ministries. The imposition of hands, then, is required only for ordination to institutional ministries.

In any case, current developments lead toward the integration of lay people into the ministries within Christian communities. This tendency is illustrated in the Roman document "*Ministeria quaedam*" from The Dogmatic Constitution of the Church, which, in spite of certain reservations, establishes ministries, in addition to the diaconate, which can be filled by non-ordained lay people. The presence of these new ministries opens new areas for reflection on the difficulties faced by young churches.

It is important to point out a decisive fact: The new understanding of the church since Vatican II presumes a greater awareness of the ecclesial meaning of Christian ministry. Besides, the new light shed by these lay ministries in a church inspired by the Spirit enhances the role of the laity within the ministerial structure. Qualification for ministry can no longer be determined simply by the laying-on of hands. Contemporary ecclesiology and the biblical theology of charisms both demand a redistribution of ministries. This redistribution of ministries, however, can *not* be treated as a "provisional, conservative step"—it is not merely a matter of letting lay people exercise certain functions as substitutes in the absence of clergy. That would not be innovation, but rather a return to the past when the power of the "orders" was the sole criterion for ministry in the church. To reduce lay people to simple auxiliaries of the clergy is to ignore their charisms and the Spirit who is the source of their ministries.[7]

Today baptism and confirmation offer a field of action for lay people. The downplaying of these sacraments has led to a form of clericalism that denies any ministry at all to the faithful. Yet perhaps we too unconsciously continue to be victims of this same mentality, particularly whenever proposals are made to solve the problem of the lack of priests in the young churches.

At one time it was thought that the revival of the diaconate would put an end to some of the difficulties experienced by dioceses with a shortage of priests. Later, when celibacy was questioned, the ordination of married men was seen a possible solution. A number of people are currently proposing this solution as a genuine last resort for young churches. It continues to tempt and seduce them even though the Roman Synod of 1971 refused to allow episcopal conferences to admit married men to the priesthood. While Paul VI was willing to consider the question, he did not conceal his personal opinion, which was unfavorable. On February 2, 1970, he wrote to Cardinal Villot:

> We cannot hide the fact that such an eventuality gives rise to grave reservations on Our part. Would it not be, among other things, a very dangerous illusion to believe that such a change

in the traditional discipline could, in practice, be limited to local cases where there is a real and extreme need? Would it not be a temptation to others to look in this direction for an apparently easier solution to the current shortage of vocations?[8]

The hierarchy tends to insist obstinately on resolving the question of ministries at the hierarchical level. I do not intend to discuss the issue of priestly celibacy; instead I want only to reduce the number of obstacles facing our communities. One such problem is the tragedy of Catholics who are no longer nourished by the Cross and the presence of the Risen One because the celebration of the Eucharist is tied to the obligation of celibacy. Is the Lord's Supper an occasional privilege granted by the Roman authority, or is it a gift of God to God's people? The requirement of celibacy was imposed on the ministers of worship following the Old Testament practice of the Levites. Why should this requirement eliminate the possibility of Eucharistic life among the increasing number of congregations without priests? Our churches should ask themselves these questions before God, examining their souls and consciences in the light of the gospel of grace.

The shortage of priests will be felt even more deeply as long as the pattern of priesthood established by the Council of Trent continues—a pattern that was adapted to a particular time of the church and to religious and theological traditions that are not ours. In other words, the young churches are not without vocations—what they lack is imagination. The new Christian communities can never be truly themselves unless they invent new forms of ecclesial life, free from a morbid dependence on foreign personnel. And, in my opinion, neither the ordination of permanent deacons nor the admission of married men to the priesthood is an original or bold solution.

The document on ministries from Vatican II envisioned functions for lay people that seemed, at that time, to require the restoration of the permanent diaconate. Thus the office of lector is no longer limited to the mere reading of Holy Scripture during Mass, but includes different forms of the Service of the Word. Similarly, the office of acolyte can be understood to include the ministry of distributing communion in liturgical assemblies without priests. In these circumstances, what need is there for permanent deacons? Are they to be "super-laity" or "mini-priests"? It is certain they would not want to be either. Even at the time of Vatican II, they occupied a difficult position, caught between a laity demanding more responsibilities and a clergy who accused the laity of "torpedoing" its prerogatives. Today deacons are most often married and earn a salary outside the church. Faced with a redistribution of ministries, they would have even more trouble defining themselves. We must soon realize that ordination to the diaconate is not necessary to fulfill new functions in the community.

In reality, it cannot be denied that the diaconate appears to be a clerical institution. Besides, promotion of the diaconate seems to have been too closely linked to the reduced numbers of clergy. In the words of Joseph Moingt:

> The first priority must be the needs of the faithful and of the Church as a whole. And what the Church needs today is to extend, to increase and diversify the channels of communication and the responsibilities within itself. The distribution of ministries must be understood within this perspective.[9]

Leadership within the Christian Community

The question of ministries should be addressed in terms of the situation and needs of Christian communities, and not as part of the crisis of the clergy. Any "clerical" solution to the problem of ministries in local churches seems to me to be backward and out-of-date. The same is true for the ordination of married men, a proposal that appears to be progressive, but does not go to the heart of the matter. In fact, the needs of autonomous communities should dominate our study of Christian ministries.

Christian communities in Africa have no future unless they can trust their own internal dynamics, their ongoing ability to respond to challenges, and their on-going capacity to face all their crises and to make full use of community resources and potential. Ecclesiastical institutions within these communities must undergo radical changes. They are still branded by a form of clerical imperialism that has inhibited their ability to innovate and stunted the growth of the laity. The vision of a Christian community incarnate in the life of a people requires that the community have full autonomy in organizing itself. From now on, instead of imposing more rules, we need to let each community work out its own direction. The emergence of such communities calls for a tremendous effort to decentralize. We must root the centers of decision-making in the local communities if they are going to truly express their faith in terms of their culture. If we want to liberate the gospel so that it can give rise to new forms in each socio-cultural context, we must start with communities that want to be responsible and self-sufficient. Research on ministries is tightly linked to reflection on these communities, which must be freed from rigid forms of organization with no roots in indigenous traditions.

Just imagine the types of liturgy that could be created to celebrate Christian funerals in the communities of a village or an urban quarter! Too often the people have nothing more to do than recite the rosary or sing old hymns. When funeral liturgies are developed in the African context, they must give a more active role to lay people, both men and women.

We should also consider bringing back the practice of confessing sins to a lay person when there is no alternative. This practice, considered by Aquinas to be a form of sacrament, was used in the West until the beginning of the fifteenth century.[10] Many African Christians live in precarious situations. Isolation, impassable roads, drought, and famine all force them to fall back on their own resources. Yet couldn't they benefit from this earlier practice of confession that has been eclipsed by discussion of the institutional priesthood?

Similarly we need to rethink the role of the presidency of these communities in relation to the ministry of the sacraments, particularly the Eucharist. A community president often has a religious function that is fully recognized by the bishop and in no way restricted to an ordained minister. If the ministry of the president of the community is recognized and there is a need (as often there is in the transitory situation of many African churches), why can't the president also be authorized to preside at the Eucharist when the community gathers together? This practice would accent the "official" character of the Eucharist, rather than the "power" qualifying a person to exercise this ministry. Then the criterion for carrying out sacramental functions would no longer necessarily be the laying-on of hands, but rather communion with the visible center of unity in the local church. If the link with the ministry of unity is preserved, the communion of the entire church with the ministry of Christ through the Spirit seems to justify a Eucharist without a priest. Research on this question is imperative today in young churches so that they can respond to the spiritual and pastoral needs of their local communities. The *bakambi* in Zaire have tried to do just this.[11]

Perhaps it is not necessary to wait for the church to open up new ways to the priesthood. The lack of an ordained minister should not condemn a church to wither away. The basic problem for young churches is "localization," which is dependent, in the final analysis, on the question of ministries. Neither indigenous clergy nor a massive presence of foreign missionaries makes a local church. It was formerly thought that the establishment of an indigenous hierarchy marked the final stage in the "implantation" of the church in mission countries. This clerical solution is appropriate for a missiology based on an ecclesiology of *law*. However, as a result of Vatican II, we now understand that:

> The Church is not truly established and does not fully live, nor is it a perfect sign of Christ unless there is a genuine laity existing and working alongside the hierarchy. . . . Therefore, from the foundation of a church very special care must be taken to form a mature Christian laity.[12]

The Council goes on to insist that if local churches are to be worthy of the name, they must have "qualified ministers . . . prepared in good time and in a manner that is in keeping with the needs of each church."[13] Here the use of the word "minister" must not be restricted to the so-called traditional priestly functions. Similarly, when it is said that a particular church should supply its own ministers, that should not be understood to mean only priests. According to the Council, "From the start the Christian community should be so organized that it is able to provide for its own needs as far as possible."[14]

A number of ministries are needed so that a local church can develop. An organization of communities that gives the laity its proper place in these ministries will go far to solve our problem. In other words, we must stop imposing on young churches solutions that do not respond to their deep hopes and anxieties. We must turn away from the beaten paths of traditional theology and explore new directions. Above all we need to *imagine* new solutions that do not simply copy former models, which are too marked by the historical characteristics of a particular period of Christian life. Truly basic reflection, open to questions from young Christian communities, may show a way out of the current impasses.

In reality, our biggest problem is not getting more ordained priests. Rather it is a question of having the whole church be a servant, just as all Christians are deacons of their brothers and sisters in the image of Christ, the servant of God and of human beings. It is less a question of ordaining men as deacons or priests than of making full use of the diaconal and priestly potential of the Christian laity. The institutional priesthood in its classic form, which inherited the rigidity of the Counter-Reformation, cannot resolve the basic problem of ministry in the church today.

The fundamental ministry of the church is the ministry of the people of God. This is why we must declericalize the whole spectrum of ministries in order to bring the laity into the ministerial work of the church. Young churches, like many others, need the existence of ministries for which one is qualified simply by baptism. The future of the churches is dependent on this. If young churches are to be autonomous, they must be "localized"—sustained by resources drawn from their own soil. That does not mean they should retire within themselves and refuse any external support, even if it is non-alienating. It does mean that local churches should stand on their own feet in nations that have come of age. In one sense, the admission of lay people to the various ministries is not only a test of the maturity of young churches, but also an essential condition if the faith is going to be implanted and expressed in the culture and language of a given people.

We must respond to the needs of our communities through innovation. Our churches must always move in the direction of creation. Our task is not to administer the institutions of Christianity but to advance the future. Everything is yet to be done, and nothing is decided in advance. With the guidance of the Spirit, we must create new ministries and perhaps restore some former ministries. On the other hand, additional ministries must spring forth from life itself through a renewal of Tradition (not to be confused with the variety of traditions). Re-establishing the importance of the laity in the context of a renewed theology of charisms provides young churches with a way to localize ministries. This new situation is already spurring local churches on to a new awareness of themselves, with the rights of questioning and experimenting given them by Vatican II. The lack or shortage of priests is a purifying test that obliges the churches to make full use of the resources of creation given them by the Spirit.

Notes

1. "Decree on the Missionary Activity of the Church," II.15 in *Vatican Council II: The Conciliar and Post Conciliar Documents*, edited by Austin Flannery (Northport, NY: Costello, 1975), p. 831.

2. Ibid., IV.23, *Vatican Council II*, p. 840.

3. "Dogmatic Constitution of the Church," IV.33, *Vatican Council II*, p. 390.

4. Ibid., IV.35, 391.

5. Ibid., IV.33, 390.

6. See Yves Congar, "Ministères et structuration de l'Église," *Maison-Dieu* 102 (1976): 18.

7. See J. Moingt, "Les ministères dans l'Église," *Études* (September 1972): 273-274.

8. "Reaffirming the Tradition of Priestly Celibacy," in *The Pope Speaks* 1 (1970): 43.

9. Moingt, *op. cit.*, p. 291.

10. See Yves Congar, *Jalons pour une théologie du laïcat* (Paris: Cerf, 1961), pp. 301-305.

11. *Bakambi* refers to the institution of trained lay pastors in the diocese of Kinshasa (Zaire) and some few others.

12. "Decree on the Missionary Activity of the Church," III.21, *Vatican Council II*, p. 838.

13. Ibid., III.20, p. 837.

14. Ibid., II.15, p. 829.

Part II

Faith at the Grassroots

Chapter 5

The Health of Those
without Dignity

Faith touches on the totality of existence and all of its problems. Thus, when faith seeks to understand itself, to verify itself and to account for itself in Africa, it must begin with the people's struggle to escape from the hellish circle in which they risk being permanently imprisoned. We must look at faith, then, at the ground level and clarify the paths faith can take in the structures of daily life. Africans are more and more preoccupied by social problems; the challenges of daily life crowd in on believers. A recent study showed that health is their priority (75%)—even before family (48%) or job security (33%).[1] Are the churches responding effectively to this general concern? How should we interpret current efforts to develop a system of health care that would be an alternative to the customary practices used in Africa?

The Medical System and the Social System

Any steps taken in the area of health care always serve a social and economic system that remains their point of reference. Before the independence movement in Africa, medical care was inseparable from the colonial policy of the European powers. A handbook on hygiene for students in Dahomey contained this text, redolent of the colonial era:

The White needs palm oil, and the palm tree does not grow in his cold country; he also needs cotton, maize, and so on. If you die, who will climb the palm tree, who will extract the oil, who will carry it to the factories? The administration needs taxes; if your children do not live, who will pay the taxes? That is why it spends money to educate doctors and to buy the heifers to produce the vaccine. As you plant a grain of corn to harvest many ears, so the government spends a little to harvest taxes which will be that much bigger with more inhabitants in Dahomey.[2]

Nothing could be clearer! The creation of wealth in the colonies is dominated by the question of manpower, which, in turn, depends on health assistance for the native peoples. Medical work must preserve the labor force that is necessary to exploit the potential value of the colonies. In the words of Albert Sarrault, Colonial Minister of France in 1912:

Medical aid . . . is our duty. But more than that, one could also say that it is our most immediate interest, the one that is most down-to-earth. For the whole work of colonization, the whole need to create wealth is overshadowed in the colonies by the question of manpower.[3]

Thus clinics and hospitals, vaccination programs, and hygiene have all been integrated into an overall system of domination. Exploitation of the colonies is nothing else than this. The irruption of capitalism in African agriculture forces the laborers, the land, and the health of the people into the constraints of a profit-making economy, breaking down the structures of traditional societies, creating unequal exchanges, and marginalizing the people. Medical care is thus central to the colonial apparatus; it is linked to tax collection and to the promotion of growing crops for export, consequently creating Africa's present food shortages that grow each day. Colonial medical work is in no sense a humanitarian or charitable enterprise. People cannot grow cotton or produce palm oil unless they are in good health. The aim is to preserve indigenous populations to ensure a profit on foreign investment.

During the colonial period, the provision of health services was controlled in the same way as forced labor. Public authorities intervened unilaterally and the people passively obeyed. The police became the best assistants of the colonial doctors. Through their efforts, epidemics of smallpox, bubonic plague, and yellow fever disappeared or diminished. The system worked. Yet the people understood nothing of the principles they were asked to follow. Regulations were issued without instruction or explanation. Yet the people obeyed. People let themselves be vaccinated because it was required, but without knowing why. The health of the people was protected without their knowledge and often against their wishes. Illiterate peasants, farm laborers, office workers, women, and children were manipulated by sophisticated knowledge and techniques whose meaning and results totally escaped them. Everything happened as if, in fact, the good health of the natives was the business of the "Whites," just as were tax collection and forced labor in the fields of the chief of police.

After decolonization, the situation has scarcely changed. On the contrary, according to a brief analysis of the socio-economic problems of health in the African context, it has gotten worse. In spite of all official declarations, nothing demonstrates that the current national system of health care is oriented toward a society that shares power and responsibility. A tendency toward "medicalization" makes poor populations a part of the world market, increasing their sense of resignation, and their dependence on the transnational corporations. It also reflects a socio-economic system in which health care is in danger of becoming the privilege of an élite. Who could possibly claim that the current medical system provides service to peasants or manual laborers in the slums? Does it contribute to enhancing the status of the mother, or acknowledge the key role African women play in educating children and in agricultural production? Or is this élitist medical care monopolized by some social groups for their own benefit—even though it consumes the scanty resources allocated to the health budget?[4]

In many regions, the entire economy is dominated by one single cash crop grown for export, and nutritional concerns have no role in agricultural planning. Agricultural priorities, investments, research, industry, transportation, and the management of peasants are all determined by the wishes and the interests of the large agribusinesses. In Cameroon where 22% of the young children suffer from chronic malnutrition,[5] corrupt officials speculate in agricultural products. In a single transaction, bureaucrats can make sums of money that field workers could not dream of earning during their entire miserable existence as the "wretched of the earth."

We should take another look at infant mortality rates in relation to "agricultural modernization," which is often part of economic and cultural colonization. The peasants always pay the price. The low productivity of agriculture is not explained solely by supposed "peasant mentalities," but equally by the systematic use of instruction, institutions and plans to disparage everything that is "traditional," the disruption of agrarian economies by inducements to grow one crop for export, the shortcomings of agricultural research, and the weakness of minimum price policies and infrastructures. These socio-economic, cultural, and political realities are the responsibility of the surrounding world rather than the peasant communities.

We must question the demagogic use of slogans like "HEALTH FOR ALL!" within a society living on one cash crop, in poor housing, and with the dilemmas caused by development. Because of these factors, the society is incapable of responding to problems of nutrition and health.[6] Food shortages result not so much from natural calamities or disasters caused by climate as from the policies of domination over the peasants.[7] Illness caused by malnutrition, which raises infant mortality rates, cannot be attributed solely to ignorance, dietary taboos, or a "primitive" mentality. The paucity of cash income in rural areas makes saving difficult or impossible, and thus worsens living and health conditions for many families. Taxes and arbitrary assessments absorb what little cash peasants earn. Is adequate nutrition for all possible in a society where gross disparities of wealth are built into the system, and where peasant families are reduced to using meat and fish for no more than seasoning?

But this situation is not the result of chance. Today the wealth of our countries is coopted by those who are cunning in diverting public goods to their own profit. As a result, a gulf yawns between the living standard of the comfortable minority of the "haves" and that of the disinherited majority.

In a book on African underdevelopment based on Cameroon,

Philippe Hugon observed that the political bourgeoisie had an income of from ten to one hundred times that of the masses, while it exercised no useful economic function whatsoever.[8] According to Hugon, the privileged class (2%, or 50,000 wage earners) earned an annual income of fifty billion Cameroonian francs (CFA) or one million CFA apiece, roughly $4,000 per person in 1968. Meanwhile, 2,100,000 workers of the rural masses (88% of the population) collectively earned sixty billion CFA, or under 30,000 CFA apiece, roughly $120 per person. After independence we find ourselves in a situation where the gap between rich and poor is ever-widening. Because inequities in consumption correspond to inequalities in income, the preferential allotment of resources and easy desk jobs to a tiny minority creates differences in the realms of health, nutrition, and housing that are felt each day.

The low social status of the peasants in comparison with the bourgeois office holders definitely has an effect on the health of individuals and social groups. But the poor health of the peasants is just one result of our system of social organization where the prosperity of a small number of people cannot hide the misery of many. In Africa, in general, the rural economy supports the burden of economic growth by producing cash crops for export, which permits both the collection of taxes at home and the accumulation of foreign currency. We must be aware of health problems in a context where African leaders dream of matching the pomp and luxury of the "Élysée" in France, while their people are sinking in the misery of huts and make-shift housing. On national holidays barrels of champagne are drunk in African capitals while millions of families lack safe drinking water and are condemned to live with parasitic diseases that weaken their constitution and slow down agricultural development.[9]

In the last analysis, the poor health and nutrition of low-income families are dependent on their low standard of living; this standard of living is created, in turn, by all the mechanisms that overexploit the labor of peasants. In this way, infectious diseases are closely linked to the economy, which has not been restructured from the bottom up to respond to the social needs of the majority. In our cities the crowding of seven to ten people in the same room encourages promiscuity and results in contagious diseases. Even in the absence of epidemics, the lack of facilities in slums worsens the health of urban populations. In Cameroon, Yaoundé, the capital, has a high incidence of diseases that are transmitted through the water supply. A study of hygienic problems in the slums of Douala, the largest city, has shown the extent of medical problems associated with poor living conditions.[10] The unhealthiness of housing conditions, the lack of clean drinking water, the long distances from wells or public taps, the accumulation of garbage—all contribute to a type of society built around increasing inequalities. Electricity and clean drinking water have become actual luxuries for the urban poor. This disparity is even greater between the islands of prosperity in the cities, and the fragile situation in the rural areas.

We must underline the inadequacies of state capitalism in the domain of health care. On the one hand, it offers incentives for investment to foreign financial groups, including tax abatements and the right to repatriate profits. On the other hand, it shows little concern for the equitable redistribution of wealth. The pitiful misery of clinics in the bush and the inadequacy of sanitary facilities expose a model of development that is wholly oriented toward the outside world and abandons the most important part of the population. An analysis of health care budgets exposes the indifference of African political régimes to improving the living conditions of the peasants who make up over 80% of the population.

The national fund for social security, for example, is reserved solely for government employees.[11] This restriction reflects a health policy that generally benefits the minority who seek to appropriate the national resources. The consumerism of the élite and the fraudulent practices of the administrative middle class illustrate the methods by which the national wealth is being redistributed. The bulk of the available resources are reserved for the functioning and upkeep of the government apparatus with its obvious class bias. Although health problems touch the vital interests of every African today, the decisions made by a small fraction of people in positions of power ultimately eliminate the marginalized populations.

In general, a class-oriented economic policy, structured and operated on the state level through large monopolistic organizations (which are, in turn, centralized and bureaucratic) always favors the urban conglomerates. For the city is where the intellectual élite gather, along with the bureaucrats of the public and private sectors. They form an entire social stratum of people who possess neither capital nor the means of production, but who still hold decision-making power about their use. They reap substantial advantages and can buy whatever is in vogue at the time. The logic of these economic choices—choices that absorb the largest part of the state's expenditures—gives far lower priority to social expenditures: housing, cultural programs, health care, and social infrastructures. The only two exceptions are public education and propaganda. In a situation like this, how can we talk about "social justice" that truly corresponds to the dreams of the majority of the people?

Not only the peasants suffer. Socio-professional groups with low incomes must subtract medical expenses from their family food budget, which is usually barely above the acceptable minimum. Programs of health care are abandoning the countryside and the outlying areas of cities; within the cities, medical care is provided almost wholly by hospitals or private clinics. Private health care establishments prefer to locate in areas where the farming population has an adequate level of purchasing power, as in the coffee-growing regions of western Cameroon and the cocoa-growing regions of the central south. Meanwhile, the state concentrates its efforts on building and modernizing hospitals in the big cities. In a country where two-thirds of the population belongs to the lowest income sector, the medical structure itself is clearly linked to the interests of the ruling classes. Health care remains, in large part, nothing but a medical service for government employees.[12]

In 1973, 290 physicians worked in the Cameroon, and 76 of these were technical assistants. Because more than half were concentrated in Yaoundé and Douala, the two largest cities, the ratio of doctors to population is not as significant as one might be led to believe. While the ratio corresponds in the strict sense of the word to the standards of the World Health Organization, the concentration of doctors in the big cities, and especially the capital, is a phenomenon that illustrates the inequities between rural zones and urban complexes. The same can be said for the number of hospital beds.[13] In our society, the lack of hygiene in public health facilities, the risk of contagion, and the danger of fecal contamination are greater than the likelihood of getting proper medical care!—which remains the privilege of the wealthy minority.[14]

The years since independence have witnessed the collapse of health services. Medications available in the market are priced beyond the reach of the masses because of their very weak buying power. Many hospitals, in effect, become distribution centers for prescriptions. Sick people who have been able to see a doctor and get a hospital bed must supply their own blankets, dressings, and medications, if they can find them. The increasing number of private clinics reinforces the unfair character of the current medical system.

While the professional conscience of the medical profession has abandoned the public hospitals, the privileged are cared for in the best clinics in Europe, at the expense of the unfortunate peasant. The systematic abandonment of health facilities reflects the inability of the medical system to promote a policy of health care that meets the needs of the working people. Not only does the style of operation and administration of most of the state machinery immobilize many innovative proposals from their inception; the sheer bulk of the hierarchical apparatus that administers health care also prevents it both from responding to the needs of the highest priority sectors, and from devising new responses to problems of health care for the majority.

The profile of medical care that emerges, in conformity with the whole of the administrative system, is one of a medical practice controlled by a medical hierarchy that administers health care as a technical undertaking. Under this system, medical care is unable to expand into an organization created by the initiatives of the people themselves. Such a self-directed organization could lead to rethinking the whole manner of practicing medicine, and could begin to demystify the role of doctors who set themselves up as mandarins as soon as they graduate from the university. At present, their "medical power" is the basis for their participation in the social power of the state bourgeoisie. Thus, the medical system implanted by colonialism is perpetuated.

It is true that this medical structure has been questioned in some countries. In Tanzania a social system called *Ujamaa* has rejected the claim to prestige of ultramodern hospitals that were reserved for the privileged urban classes and whose operation absorbed most of the available foreign exchange. Villages are now invited to build their own clinics, and the government assigns them health workers as far as resources and personnel permit. Emphasis is placed on preventive services and anything that can improve hygiene and dietary habits. In 1973 the national campaign for "PEOPLE IN GOOD HEALTH" was integrated into literacy classes for adults and reinforced by radio; it was extended in 1974 with the theme "NUTRITION IS LIFE." At the same time, a big effort was made to provide drinking water for the countryside. The provision of pure water, Nyerere said, "shall be from now on a major priority for the Party and the government, just as it is for the people directly concerned."[15]

But elsewere, in general, "class" medicine is being entrenched under our eyes—medical care is reserved for an urban minority, abandoning both the rural masses and the populations of black shantytowns to endemic diseases. Thus peasants always feel that, even though forced labor has been abolished, they are still not masters of their own destiny; rather they are the guinea pigs or victims of endlessly repeated experiments, and prey to an administrative bureaucracy swollen with managerial groups. They can see no difference between colonialism and the new régimes. Perhaps it is only that the masters have changed color. Although more than 80% of the population lives in rural areas, allocations for health care are made in terms of the large urban centers. In this situation, the churches must examine their options for health care in light of their commitment in faith to the heart of the present problems of our society.

Christian Missions and Health Programs

An inquiry into the relationship between Christian missions and health programs is inevitable. In one sense, the history of Christian missions in Africa is inseparable from medical and health programs.[16] In time, each mission acquired a clinic as regularly as it built a school. The arrival of religious sisters to staff the clinic was usually the determining factor. Two-thirds of the religious congregations operating in Africa were dedicated to medical work. Albert Schweitzer popularized this image of the missionary doctor. In the end, each ecclesiastical jurisdiction built at least one hospital, and many missionaries felt themselves able to disinfect a wound or hand out aspirin or doses of quinine. For more serious cases, though, they turned to the clinic or to the doctor at the nearest hospital. Mission vehicles often served as ambulances. In some parts of Africa, especially in the countryside, Western medical care was usually available only in missionary facilities. Quite often the missions also served as dispensaries or hospitals where there were no actual clinics founded by religious orders and staffed by men and women belonging to missionary societies. These were often solid establishments with devoted and conscientious personnel. However there was still a certain ambiguity about them.

In Moslem territories, missions do not have the right to consider conversion, or undertake general works of social assistance such as schools, clinics, and hospitals, and other forms of indirect apostolates. Social works, which are publicly recognized as meritorious, are used by various confessions to promote their causes. In this context, the quality of one's faith can be confirmed by effectiveness in healing. Although many missionaries have no intention of using medical treatment as a means of conversion to Christianity, the connivance of evangelization with medical work arouses the mistrust of various African sectors. This mistrust was especially prevalent during the colonial period when medicine and mission seemed to have the same goal. In his book *Kel-lam, Son of Africa*, Father Carré has his hero say:

> Whites, you see, are very cunning. They have created many miseries for us with their forced labor and their taxes, and then to comfort us, they send us their brother the doctor to care for us and their father to talk to us about God.

Thus the salvation of the soul and efforts to heal are both interpreted as consolation within a system of oppression and domination. But what was the real effect in the missions, after the epidemic of building dispensaries ended? Do today's medical practices help maintain mechanisms that continue to produce conditions of misery and sickness? Or can efforts to promote health care for all the people become an enterprise of real salvation? Is a break with the present medical system, which favors an élite, a step in the direction of the Kingdom of God—even if we don't transform health facilities into chapels or catechetical stations? A fresh look at biblical sources can provide some guidelines in answering these questions.

Sickness and Sin in the Bible

We must remember that sickness is usually viewed in the Bible as the result of personal sin (Eccles. 6:2-4; 38:9-10). As in the cases of Saul (I Sam. 16:14) and Uzziah the leper (2 Kings 15:5), sickness is a punishment of God; and the sick person pays the penalty for his or her sins (Job 18:13). This opinion was widespread among Jews up to the time of Jesus. The instance of the man who was blind from birth is a good example of this viewpoint. Jesus' disciples ask him, "Rabbi, who sinned, this man or his parents, for him to have been born blind?" (John 9:1-2). This question illustrates perfectly the conception that was current in the ancient world of a direct link between sin and physical ailments (Exod. 9:1-12; Ps. 38:2-6; Ez. 18:20). As a corollary, the whole tragedy of a righteous person struck by sickness appears as a sign of divine love. The first Christian communities cited this teaching of the old sages of Israel: "Suffering is part of your training; God is treating you as sons and daughters," writes the author of the Epistle to the Hebrews (Prov. 3:11-12; Heb. 12:7). The biblical revelation looks beyond physical sickness towards a reality that touches the human heart. The true malady is the sin that is congenital in every human being: "You know I was born guilty, a sinner from the moment of conception" (Ps. 51:5).

The New Testament also establishes a link between sickness and the demonic (Luke 13:11, 16). In acts that are inseparable, Jesus heals the sick and chases away demons to manifest his victory over sin (Luke 13:32). He grants pardon to the paralytic waiting to be healed before he heals him (Luke 5:18-20). The sick man healed at the pool of Bethzatha is invited to change his life (John 5:14). Jesus asks faith of the man blind from birth (John 9:35-39). In general, faith is a prerequisite for healing. The importance of this healing ministry of Jesus—whether by touch (Mark 1:41; Matt. 9:29; Luke 14:4; Mark 7:35), the laying on of hands (Mark 8:23-26; Luke 13:13), or a simple word (Luke 7:7)—should be emphasized when describing the mission of Jesus (Matt. 4:24; Acts 10:38).

These collections of healing narratives are part of a larger body of teaching wherein each story takes its meaning from a specific context. The healing of the lepers raises questions about the laws of purity and impurity (Lev. 13:9-16; 14:1-32) that exclude various social categories from the community (Matt. 9:10). In rehabilitating those whom official Judaism rejects and condemns, Jesus breaks down the frontiers of ritual that separate individuals or peoples from each other. Healing reintegrates a human being into society at large. Jews understood from these teachings that people could be saved even if they lived outside the official cultural community.

Jesus' exorcisms seem linked to the power of God delivering the people from the monsters of the first days (Ps. 89:9-10). Jesus the healer is revealed in the Servant spoken of by Isaiah (Matt. 8:16-17; 12:15-21), and the songs of the suffering Servant are the context within which the healings of the gospels can be understood. When Jesus cures "all kinds of diseases and sickness among the people" (Matt. 4:23), he appears as the new Moses (Acts 3:22; 7:37; Deut. 18:15), the Messiah announced by the prophets and awaited by the poor and oppressed.

The recollection of healing done on the sabbath assumes considerable importance within the Jewish culture (Luke 13:15; 14:3-5). In effect, the healing of the man with a withered hand does not extol the power of Jesus as a miracle-worker, but announces instead liberation from slavery to the law. From their perspective of resurrection, the new communities read and interpreted many healing narratives in which paralytics, the sick, and the dead were raised up (John 11:1-44; 5:26-29). They understood that the resurrection expected at the last day (Dan. 12:2; 2 Macc. 12:44; John 5:28-29; 6:39-40; Acts 24:15) was already possible in this world. The signs performed by Jesus are not to be reduced to proofs of his divinity, as a facile apologetic once thought; rather, they reveal the presence of the Kingdom in the world. They announce a new age and fulfill the messianic hope. Jesus is not a miracle-worker whose power overthrows the laws of nature, but the one who roots salvation in the web of history—it is the fullness of this salvation for which the church is waiting.

Whenever a person is reborn to life by the force of the gospel operating fully through the word and actions of Jesus, salvation is available in "bodily" form. As Jesus heals, he reveals to humanity here below in the flesh that world where "there will be no more death, and no more mourning or sadness" (Rev. 21:4). By healing the sick, Jesus places himself in the messianic tradition where the righteous await total and universal redemption. He announces and anticipates the remaking of the cosmos; he opens to humanity a perspective of the time when death will be conquered (1 Cor. 15:52-55). We must remember that the basic message of the gospel is the redemption of our body (Rom. 8:23).

The human race is not saved independently of the universe. "The whole creation is eagerly waiting for God's revelation. . . . From the beginning till now the entire creation . . . has been groaning in one great act of giving birth"; yet it "still retains the hope of being freed . . . from its slavery to decadence" (Rom. 8:20-24). The manifestation of the glory of the Risen One will cover the entire cosmos. The association of the physical universe with the glorification of the children of God is a corollary of the Christian faith. In this context, human health appears as one dimension of the salvation whose fullness we await in a glorious future. Strictly speaking, to be healed—that is, to be delivered from evil—is in itself to be saved. Humanity is invited to enter into that state of creation marked by the saving power of the Resurrection.

The coming of Jesus ushers in the nearness of the Kingdom (Mark 1:15). From that time, sickness (which, in the Jewish tradition, and especially in the book of Job, appears as a curse and a trial sent by Yahweh) points toward the hope of a bodily re-creation, involving both the physical world and individuals themselves in their relationships to others and to God. The healings performed by Jesus point the way to a second creation of the entire universe within our history. These healings, the signs of the Kingdom of God in the here-and-now of human history, attest to the presence of messianic salvation. "Go back and tell John what you hear and see; the blind see again, and the lame walk, lepers are cleansed, and the deaf hear, and the dead are raised to life and the Good News is proclaimed to the poor" (Matt. 11:4-5).

In the gospels, we see how the realities of the world are lifted up to become the sacrament or the privileged language of the transformations brought about by the Messiah. The many forms of deliverance signified by healing in the gospels define the liberation of humanity through Jesus Christ. They allow us to hear and see the liberating activity of the Messiah on behalf of the poor and oppressed. The incarnation is the time when God decisively announces the gospel and frees the captives (Luke 4:18-19). How can this time of God be actualized in contemporary African society, apart from reference to questions of health? What's the use of a "medicine" coopted for the benefit of wealthy minorities, when the "*lives*" of those neglected by its progress are stuck in structures of inequity and injustice?

Underdevelopment: The Locus of God's Healing Will

The critical situation in Africa today requires us to reexamine the theological or religious tradition that interprets the universe of sickness by referring to a myth of punishment or fault. As we view the situation of humanity in the universe, there is certainly no question of abandoning our understanding of the drama of sin. But today we do need to understand the archaic link formerly drawn between sickness and guilt. So we are led to question the Word of God, to redefine and interpret the tragedy of sickness. We are led to give concrete historical responses to this infidelity to the covenant, whose effects were seen by Jews of that time as curses and punishment.

The Bible suggests a reciprocity between individuals and society, in which individuals endanger the community by their faults and, in turn, collective sin is echoed by sicknesses within the bodies of individuals. This dynamic of socio-religious relations portrays the drama of sin and salvation (Rom. 5:12-21). But if we situate the heart of this drama in the inaccessible origins of humanity, we confine its disorder to the realm of the inner life, and treat sickness as nothing more than the effect and consequence of original sin. In doing so, we gloss over the actual opacity of sickness, and do not accept its real forms. We transfer its burden to a realm of unquestioning faith and passive resignation. If we consider the violence being done to life in the conditions in which we live, and localize it in the invisible relationship of the soul with God, we spiritualize it to a dangerous degree. We "sacralize" it. We constantly risk transforming sin into a structure of mythical existence against which we can do nothing, except ritually in the church through the sacramental and "religious" activity that is used to symbolize our faith. Such conceptions hardly prepare us to confront the tragedy of our history or to become masters of our destiny. Prayer and sacramental rites, the imposition of hands, and exorcisms can be dangerous alibis, and a type of refuge from the harsh realities of today's life and society—especially if we remember that psychological states of possession are a type of disturbance characteristic of a time of crisis and cultural change.

During the time of Jesus Christ, sickness was identified with the domination of evil forces, and healing was seen as deliverance from their hold. Can such an interpretation be valid in our time? Or does our situation require another interpretation and another practice of our faith that is committed to the struggle on behalf of humanity? The gospel proposes a connection between sickness and possession. Can this same link indicate historical and cultural models of evil and violence that hide in the contradictions of our own society?

We must not reduce all the disorders of the world in our time to illustrations of a paradigm beyond history, or manifestations of a metaphysical catastrophe at the very beginning of time. We must learn to listen anew to what the Word of God says about sin in each person, place, and historical situation. We are called to give witness to the hope of the Kingdom amid the distress of this life. As humanity, we need to tell God "No," given these specific historical, social, economic, political, or cultural conditions. First we must take note of the structures of an ill-made world that contradict the will of God for humanity and the world, beginning with the ravages of these structures on individuals and human groups. That is precisely what we are doing when we dismantle the mechanisms of sickness and the laws that establish them.

An analysis of the socio-economic indicators of health in Africa reveals the mechanisms that enclose human beings in a circle of misery and sickness. Questions of nutrition and health are inseparable from the economic and social systems. Disease and malnutrition never exist by themselves; rather they are the effects or products of social organizations. The position of sickness in black Africa is a decisive reality of *our* time and of *our* historic condition. The fact of domination works behind the scenes to design our institutions, infrastructures, modes of relationships, and internal and external connections. We must abandon any ideology that makes sickness a matter of fatalism—the invasion of an imaginary "adversary" beyond human responsibility or the reach of any strategies of people living in society.

In our situation, sickness is the result of the aggression of human beings against one another; it comes from a system characterized by violence, by a pattern of impoverishment of the majority, and by the monopoly by a minority of the means to live with dignity. To insist on a link between sickness and underdevelopment means simply to recognize the contemporary connection between sickness and deprivation, between exploitation and dependency.

We must recognize one basic fact: Although analysis shows that the world is so organized that it cannot but produce underdevelopment, injustice and misery, this structure is radically incompatible with the plan of God and with the recognition of God as God. A society that condemns millions of children to malnutrition and sickness cannot possibly be part of God's plan for Africa today. It is precisely this ugly face of the "sin of the world" that the Lamb of God has assumed and carried away. We must highlight this contradiction to the will of God, starting with our own economic and social condition, and including its effects—the illness endemic in our historical and cultural environment. As we do this, we will hear the appeal to participate in the transformation of this badly made world.

Today that participation is a prerequisite for any conversion to a living relationship with God. From now on, we need a fresh hearing of the Word of God, starting with underdevelopment and its consequences, which clarifies the actual pattern of cause and effect that can no longer remain hidden. Passive acceptance of the injustice generated by a medical system that reflects present African socio-economic structures is incompatible with the true worship of God—just as is idolatry. Active resistance is an essential feature of the practice of our faith. It must begin with problems of human health and move to challenge the unjust organization of African society.

It is not just a question of a subtle form of paternalism or of condescension and pity toward the "poor blacks," both of which allow people to keep themselves at a distance. Nor is it a question of the innocence of those who provide medical care who feel they are not involved in the drama of sickness in Africa. The churches face a big temptation to take delight in providing care for the most repulsive diseases, which they do almost as if they are trying to use up their resources in works of compassion and pity. A kind of nihilism sometimes shows through this frenzy to provide care and, in the end, transforms the unfortunate into objects of care by a good Samaritan, with no concern for the economic and social schemes that are precisely the origins of the evil.

A Challenge for the Churches: Mistrust Our Motives

In order to provide the type of health care that is needed in Africa, we must dare to oppose accepted ideas and practices that deprive people of responsibility for the conditions of their existence. Vatican II reminded us that one task of the church is to awaken people to their intelligence and to the scope of their freedom. Health services become truly pastoral actions only when they help create an irreversible situation that frees people from the forces of death. Practices that deal only with the effects of illness do not contribute to this overall purpose. As Christians we must go to the roots of sickness by totally restructuring living conditions in our society. In the words of Vatican II, "there will first have to be a renewal of attitudes and far-reaching social changes" (*Gaudium et Spes* 26.2).

In a missionary context where the struggle for justice is a necessary dimension of preaching the gospel,[17] medical institutions are forced to redesign a system of health care for the people who have been neglected since independence. In the church today, we are aware of the need to defend human beings and to struggle against misery. In our countries where the economic and health situation is particularly difficult for most of our African populations, we must join people where they are, with their feet in the mud. Country people and the inhabitants of city slums are sick because they are peasants crushed by injustice and famine. It is hard to provide health care for them without leading them out of silence and without helping them escape from their forced status as outcasts— both of which close them in a circle of underdevelopment and sickness. The search for signs of the Kingdom in the concreteness of daily life must include letting their voices be heard, and helping them resist any form of passive acceptance of their environment.

How are we to live the gospel in a situation where hospitals themselves are centers of exploitation and corruption? At this very hour, it is not easy to gain admission to a public hospital, and even once admitted, patients are not treated according to their needs. Any idea of urgency evaporates. It is often difficult to get a bed, even if a disease is eating up your flesh. The rich, the "patrons," do not have the least difficulty in seeing a doctor or in finding places for themselves and their entourages. Specialists are mobilized to treat a cold or constipation if the patient is élite, while the children of the poor with no resources are dying all around because they have no money for health care. We live in a society where medicine examines not patients but their wealth, their class, their position of power in the dynamic of social relations.

Food, fruit, salad, meat, fish, and drinking water are indispensable to good health, but for many these are luxuries. The dogs guarding the villas of residential quarters are better nourished than the children of the bush. This is what must change. The struggle for health care must be placed in the context of the struggle for another society, another humanity, another system of production, another style of living together, both within the family and society as a whole. We must struggle against alienating forces and, at the same time, give back to people their responsibility for themselves and their bodies, teaching them to challenge anything that smacks of chance and destiny.

Today many African governments abdicate their responsibility to make economic and political decisions concerning nutrition. They prefer to beg now and again, thus maintaining a situation that continues to create dependencies. Should this system be supported and consolidated? Or should health care institutions promote a different system, directed to meeting the nutritional needs of every age group, rather than just pregnant women and small children? Can clinics and hospitals become centers promoting a form of agriculture that no longer enriches the rich or organizes rural development against the peasant? Questions such as these are endless! I just want to emphasize their importance in our situation where questions of health care can contribute to human development and the emergence of new forms of social organization.[18]

But we must raise questions about ourselves, before we seek out the people of the bush or the city slums to help them formulate their needs and hopes or to analyze and understand their situation as it relates to health care. We cannot ask these poor people to let us become their comrades in struggle for health without overthrowing the medical powers that always tend to become forces of oppression. People resign themselves to this situation more readily because medical care is dressed in the virtues of charity and good deeds. We cannot resist medical care determined by class, unless we proceed to what Cabral calls "class suicide"[19]—namely, what is called "conversion" in our Christian language. Does the relationship of medical personnel to sickness serve to sharpen their critical awareness, to increase their understanding, and to reinforce their determination to battle against ignorance? Or rather, does their experience of life and their involvement in the world of medicine tend to develop an awareness of their own superiority, to solidify their class awareness and their feelings of power and knowledge? It is possible to have a complete certainty that one is doing good, in a spirit of service and concern for the poor, and yet work for the victory of a system of domination, and even, in the end, lead its victims on to accept it and internalize it. We must learn to mistrust ourselves—and our good intentions.

This need for vigilance is necessary in our journey of faith. As we provide health care, we can also help create the conditions that free humanity—*if* we let ourselves be transformed through the provocative power of the gospel. For we can be "capitalists of knowledge" without even knowing it, if we are not involved in projects that are truly "apostolates of dirty hands." Such apostolates, starting with our solidarity with the poor and oppressed, lead us from an awareness of the sins of the world to transform the world and ourselves, so that faith opens our eyes to discover God present and active in all hopes and struggles for freedom and justice.

Notes

1. *Jeune Afrique* (March 12, 1980).

2. See Dominingo, Dieudonné Sedan, *La politique sanitaire au Dahomey entre les deux guerres*, Mémoire de Maîtrise VII (Paris, 1975).

3. See J. Suret-Canale, *Afrique Noire: L'Ère coloniale (1900-1945)* (Paris: Éditions Sociales, 1977), p. 505.

4. See a study by P. Robert in the *Revue Française d'Études Politiques Africaines* for April 1977.

5. See the conclusions of the *Enquête Nationale sur la Nutrition*, p. 66. For Africa as a whole, see the table of the nutritional situation in *Annuaire Jeune Afrique* (1979): 303-306.

6. For data on the links between malnutrition and the disintegration of African economies, see the thesis of J. Blanc, *Malnutrition et sous-développement* (Rome: Pontifical Gregorian Univ., 1975).

7. *Qui se nourrit de la famine en Afrique? Le dossier politique de la faim au Sahel* (Paris: Maspéro, 1974); H. Derriennic, *Famines et dominations en Afrique Noire: Paysans et éleveurs du Sahel sous le joug* (Paris:

L'Harmattan, 1977); Jacques Giri, *Le Sahel demain, catastrophe ou re-naissance?* (Paris: Karthala, 1983).

8. Philippe Hugon, *Analyse du sous-développement en Afrique Noire: L'exemple de l'économie du Cameroun* (Paris: Presses Universitaires de France, 1968).

9. This point is developed by A. Tévoèdjré in his book, *La pauvreté, richesse des peuples* (Paris: Éditions Ouvrières, 1978), pp. 69-106.

10. See the *Cameroun-Tribune*, January 30, 1980; and Y. Morel, "Rôle d'un dispensaire de quartier à Douala," in *Croyance et guérison* (Yaoundé: CLE, 1973), pp. 90-93.

11. In the *Effort Camerounais* of February 17, 1974, the minister Ayissi Mvodo explains why there are no family payments for peasants. A contrary opinion demanding them is expressed by Senga Kuo, *Effort Camerounais* of March 31, 1974.

12. Issue no. 24 of *Famille et Développement*, "Le droit à la santé pour qui?" examining primarily West Africa, very clearly shows the development of medical care for the urban minorities in the capitals on pp. 37-42; see also *Annuaire Jeune Afrique* (1979): 319.

13. For the province of North Cameroon with 2,237,257 inhabitants, in 1978/79 there was 1 doctor for every 40,350 people, compared to 31,900 in 1977/80; 1 hospital bed for 782 patients, instead of 64. And obviously, the services indicated by these numbers benefit only some of the privileged people in cities. Similar statistics for all of Cameroon can be found on pages 3 and 121 of the *World Health Statistics Annual, 1980*.

14. On the difficulties of getting access to health care in Cameroon, see an article "Les tribulations du malade" in the magazine *Perroquet* 11 (August 1979).

15. See J. K. Nyerere, *La Déclaration d'Arusha, 10 ans après* (Paris: L'Harmattan, 1978), p. 19. English edition, *The Arusha Declaration, 10 Years After* (Dar es Salaam: Government Printer, 1977).

16. See the remarks of N. Ossama, "Pratique médicale missionnaire lors de la première évangélisation," in M. Hebga, ed., *Croyance et guérison* (Yaoundé: CLE, 1973), pp. 71-85.

17. See the Synod of 1974 in *Modern Missionary Documents and Africa*, edited by Raymond Hickey (Dublin: Dominican Publications, 1982).

18. The observations of Ivan Illich on this theme remain fully relevant; see his *Medical Nemesis* (New York: Random, 1975).

19. The major works of Amilcar Cabral, a major African architect of independence from Portuguese colonialism, have been translated into English and published by Monthly Review Press (New York): *Revolution in Guinea: Selected Texts by Amilcar Cabral* (1970); *Return to the Source: Selected Speeches of Amilcar Cabral* (1974); *Unity and Struggle, Speeches and Writings of Amilcar Cabral* (1979).

Chapter 6

The Granary Is Empty

It seems that drought and famine have become an African scourge. Pictures of its victims, African children with swollen bellies and skeletal limbs, are projected throughout the world by the media. Public opinion, teams of researchers, and many different organizations are mobilized, while the Food and Agriculture Organization cries out in alarm over the seriousness of food shortages. Paradoxically, these same shortages have fed vast markets during the last fifteen years, and the industry of misery prospers!

Christians are celebrating the Eucharist while entire populations are vulnerable to the weapon of grain, and condemned to live on imported food products. Is the question of food essential to our faith? Of course! The Eucharist is not even imaginable without the fruits of the earth produced by peasants, who bring together agriculture and the celebration of the history of salvation. But can our Eucharist be called Christian if it abandons countless young people to their sad fate in regions where "the other half of the world is dying"? How can we truly be nourished by the body of Jesus Christ, while a minority is satiated, and yet each year millions of people have no food and face an empty granary? We cannot help but associate the table of the altar with the "table of the Magnificat" as did Anselme Sanon, a theologian from the Sahel.[1] Our practice of the Christian faith faces a major challenge from African men and women who agonize over where their next meal is coming from.

Our churches today expose us to the dangers of atheism each time we celebrate the Eucharist in areas where no one is working to

87

create conditions that would allow hungry people to feed themselves. The peasants in the village of Tokombéré in northern Cameroon showed us how they have been prevented from feeding their families. Before they began their Easter celebration, they recalled the events that marked their life during the year, and then they ended with a recitation of the Passion of Jesus. Bouba, the leader of the community, began:

> The farm supervisor, the chief of the district, and the sub-prefect called us all together. They told us, "Now you will pull up all the millet that you have grown in order to plant cotton." While they watched, we began to pull up our millet. Lifting our arms to heaven, each person held the stalks of millet with one hand and said, "My God, you can see that I am not the one who is doing it; my God, it's not me."

In order to understand the meaning of this gesture, we must remember that for the people of northern Cameroon, and in particular the Kirdi, millet is a gift from God. According to their tradition, it was God who told them to "Dig up the mountain and cultivate millet." Millet means life; custom forbids pulling it up. So, in this act, the peasants called God to witness that they had no part in the action. "My God, it is not me." We must remember all the elements of the scene: the millet, the peasants, the agents of the government, the administration, and above all, the invocation to God. Bouba finishes, "This is the suffering that Jesus carried for us; it was our sorrows that he bore."

"Africa Strangled": The Peasants

The drama of the Kirdi is shared by millions of African peasants who ask only to live. "We know that we are peasants, we do not want to be like the city people, the rich! We just want to live better!" This disclosure by an old man appears in a film shot by Frères des Hommes in Piala, a village in Burkina Faso. The bush people in a village lost in the immensity of the Sahel are torn between famine and "here today, gone tomorrow" development schemes. They are prisoners in a system devised elsewhere for the interests of others. These attempts at "rural modernization" actually seem to enlarge the cities and shantytowns, and endanger the productive base of the society that lies in the villages. But what else can we expect? After all, the development of these projects matches the interests of foreign capital and its "watchdogs." The axis of the African economy, from their point of view, is producing cotton, coffee, peanuts, palm oil, sugar, cocoa, and rubber.

Multinational corporations and banks have invaded a diversity of situations and political systems in Africa, and strangle the peasant men and women who comprise the majority of its people. Almost everywhere throughout the black continent, the various forms of coercive apparatus of the multinationals guarantee optimal conditions for the over-exploitation of human labor and natural resources. Although the capitalist-oriented economies dominate our societies and profit from them, it is not clear that they actually improve the lot of the African masses. René Dumont has shown how bureaucratic minorities squander foreign aid, while they exploit the peasants and ruin their land and soil.[2] And Julius Nyerere testified to the emergence of a privileged élite whose scandalous lifestyle feeds off the over-exploitation of village laborers: "The countryside produces, the city consumes."

Today the constraints of international trade have become overwhelming. African governments and social authorities, however, do have a certain freedom of initiative and action. And yet, using a surplus of export crops to extend its authority, the state seems to have allowed the growth of a managerial élite and supported a political-administrative class that oppresses the peasant masses.

While the specter of hunger and death prowls our continent, certain peasants continually say that "independence is the business of the sons of the Whites." They feel that this black minority has restored the use of a model of development for African villages that is based on exploitation. Unemployment (which has begun to affect even university graduates), malnutrition, and torture are outcomes of this control held over all of black Africa. We have been permanently reduced, it seems, to a situation where poverty and oppression surround a few islands of affluence. A multitude of the oppressed are up against an élite that always tends to reinforce its position of power by setting up a system whose results are clear. Millions of expelled citizens have been uprooted from their backgrounds and families, and become refugees in other countries.

Others live in "interior exile" within their own countries where small stirrings of opposition are nipped in the bud by repression and intimidation.

The reality of Africa—after it has been stripped of its folklore—demands attention. Twenty years of independence have not brought development, but rather developed underdevelopment. The situation becomes more serious when the state itself is the instrument of repression. It is important to understand the relationship in Africa between the government and the people. There is little effective participation of the people in public affairs, and the masses have practically no way of controlling government power, but only of applauding its use. Did God really plan that our continent be a land of oppression, poverty, and injustice? As black Africa becomes increasingly impoverished, must we close the door on hope?

The Confrontation of Cultures and the Irruption of the Poor

For more than twenty years, black priests, pastors and theologians, bush catechists and urban intellectuals, an ever-increasing number of bishops, and foreign missionaries have discussed the advent of African Christianity. The event of Pentecost makes it clear that the gospel should be lived and translated into all languages. But who has the right to impose a foreign style of living on other people? Because Christianity has failed to speak about God in a relevant manner, independent churches and sects have proliferated. We must rethink our basic faith because it has failed to enter genuinely into African life and root itself there, and because its claim to universality has been destroyed. As we bring Christianity face to face with the African reality, we must rethink God.

For some years we have reflected about our Christian faith in the context of the confrontation of cultures. If the future of Christianity lies within Africa (and many signs seem to indicate this is true), the irruption of the poor must challenge our faith as Africans. Soon the church will no longer be able to pass by "the man who fell among robbers." Our African society is sick in this same way with corruption and injustice; it is consumed by bitterness, and threatened by the clutches of famine whose very appearance strangles the whole of life. Fear paralyzes energy and initiative. People lacking the power of speech back away from their own history. They do not react to the failures of the public authorities or to the powerlessness of the parasitic middle class.

But there is a sign of hope in the ferment of small communities committed to the poor and the downtrodden. These communities' experience of the Christian faith goes beyond all those acts and rituals that are included in the indigenization of Christianity: initiation rites, the world of the invisible, the cult of ancestors, and the importance of sacrifices.

Evangelizing people shaped by a certain culture must go hand in hand with their struggle for development in all aspects of their lives. Hence, the work of our faith must be understood in reference to the overall situation in Africa today. We must deal with down-to-earth questions, and get back to ground level where the Kingdom of God is built day by day. For the hope for a new world that is built in the framework of justice, peace, and freedom is the heart of the Christian message. We must get involved in this experience and use it as our starting-point for a radical critique of all that is happening before our eyes. This is the only source of energy that will impel us to interpret Christian responsibilities in the current context of black Africa.

The irruption of the poor throughout the countries of the Third World is radically changing the mission of the church. Religious communities, pastoral workers, and lay movements are shifting their focus. New questions are being asked of theological reflection, pastoral practice, and spiritual life in many different places where the church is getting out of its traditional rut, and being born again from the dominated and exploited people. The poor and oppressed are reclaiming the Word of God and changing the structures of a world that is incompatible with God's plan. Working through historical dynamics, the poor are called by the gospel to ask hard questions and to become participants with the power to change their own living conditions.

This is all happening at a moment when the strength of the gospel is being discovered in the midst of the plundering of the Third World, the destruction of its cultures, and its relegation to a simple source of raw materials for the dominant industrial countries. This is a momentous experience of faith. Solidarity is now the business of the poor themselves, as they learn to be together in a village or a slum and work to solve their own problems and to share their life and their struggles—everything that comprises their essence and their deepest hopes. The most striking development is their will to make common cause in a dynamic directed to create a different society.

Nascent Christian communities are being built around a sharing of initiatives and projects so they can go beyond the impasses posed by development. In this way, the practice of the gospel is much closer to the reality of Africa, which today is a vast battlefield of multinational interests closely tied to life in the villages and the slums. By working in communities, people are able to come together to take charge of economic, social, and practical realities: the use of money, privately owned dispensaries, grain banks, methods of drilling wells, and so forth. We should ask ourselves if these actions of small communities aren't the best response to the impasses reached in many countries.

One thing that is clear is that the African church is still waiting to hear strong voices denounce corruption, torture, exploitation, and the oppression of the masses by a minority. Communities forming today throughout Africa will certainly make it clear that injustice and famine result above all from the acceptance of the current model of development—a model imposed on the peasants since independence. The extreme misery of the countryside and the outlying urban areas is the direct effect of a whole system of domination that forces peasants to grow cotton and other export crops even though they feed no one.

A Ministry of the Granary

What use is there in mobilizing communities unless the goal is to shelter peasants from the weapon of food? Peasant families are crushed by requirements to produce peanuts, cocoa, or cotton. That is why I deliberately chose a "ministry of the granary." African agriculture has been disrupted by its emphasis on capital. Today the question of food must again become the center of daily life—starting from an African culture that is based on granaries, and the dynamics of the revelation as it is read in Genesis through Matthew. In times of famine, God wills that humanity should be fed (Gen. 42:1-2, 43:1-2), and in the end God totally identifies with the hungry (Matt. 25:35-42).

Because the God of the gospel is revealed as the God who brings life, our faith requires us to reject any system that produces empty granaries—signs of famine and death. The message and the work of Jesus denounce exploitation of peasants, and demand new forms of relationships where people can organize themselves so that no one is deprived of the needed ration of millet. How can we speak of the Lord of Life, knowing full well that famine is the messenger of death? A look at village life in Africa today shows that it is no longer just the elderly who are near death; now children are dying of malnutrition. Is this an action of God? Does God will it? Would this still happen if people organized themselves in working groups so they could have enough food all year round? Such a project demands a clear understanding of the place of the granary in village life, of concerns for children, the relationships between men and women, the whole question of health care, and, of course, the importance of land.

The overall organizing process requires a series of mutually complementary actions. Primary-school students are taught to become the eyes of their village. After this type of training, one student observed during a discussion that, "Because they have taken away our fields, there is no place left to grow millet." Literacy training for adults is also an integral part of this project. Over a period of several weeks, groups of men and women learn to read and write using texts that show they cannot eat cotton. The newly literate can then send news to members of their family who have gone to the city, and tell them what happens in the village after a bad harvest. Their messages describe what is going on in the village, the need to speak out, the centers of decision-making, and the various groups engaged in different activities: educators, doctors, rural organizers, those in charge of agriculture, government representatives. These messages might include reflection on the theme that feeding people is a political problem.

This "ministry of the granary" has led me to a better understanding of the mechanisms operative in the cotton-growing region of northern Cameroon—the economic choices available, the strategies of the state-owned corporations, speculation in millet, and administrative corruption. (In the process, I became somewhat suspicious of the information services, which would hide the real misery of the peasants if it served their purposes.) When I worked in youth camps deep in the mountains, I glimpsed how hope could be born again in the hearts of the poor when students from second-ary schools or grammar schools returned to the villages to be with the peasants, live with them, and talk with them. The students seriously questioned the practices of the communities, and chal-lenged a system that creates hunger and yet makes "the rich richer and the poor poorer." Each year these people have less to eat, and wonder if they will continue to live so poorly, or perhaps not live at all. How can they be helped to take responsibility for eliminating the causes of famine and death so as to live the life of justice and mutual help described in the gospel? I finally realized that it is in the community itself where we experience the power of the Lord, and can celebrate God through signs of our faith.

My ministry in the north was motivated by a challenge made to me more than ten years ago by a wise old man. One evening I was in a village in the north intending to bring the Word of God to the people. Some young people had announced my arrival, saying "This is the son of Baba Simon, who is coming here to talk about God." Shortly after I began, this old man interrupted me: "Once upon a time God talked to people, but now he has fallen silent, and he has left us prey to hunger, sickness, and death."

Communities controlled by hunger and slavery *can* recover their true dignity through a peasant reading of the Bible. It can lead them to a path of liberation that will show each of them the secret of their existence and a reason for living. I feel this is what is at stake today in the searching and experimenting going on in Africa where the Spirit is working to build a church from the struggles of peasants. Today God is again speaking to the Kirdi. God's message is revealed when peasants gather together, hear anew the gospel, and recite it by heart. God speaks through their efforts to take charge of their own lives in communities that show an understanding of them-selves and work for their own evangelization.

I could cite a whole series of testimonies to show this is true, but I need only recall these words of a leader at a community meeting:

> In the beginning, children and adults came to hear the Word of God. Somebody asked, "Why are we different? Why are we so poor?" When we heard the story of Adam and Eve, people said to themselves, "We are the ones driven out of the garden to settle here in the mountains." We went on reflecting

together, trying to understand why we were so unfortunate and poor. We saw that we didn't have any water. What could we do? We sunk a well. The villagers helped us lay down the pipes and we saw the results. That was an idea that came from people working together.

Then we looked at the problem of health care. We put some people in charge and set up a health committee. We taxed ourselves to buy the basic medicines and have a small dispensary. Even though the parents of the school children had never gone to school themselves, they formed a self-help committee to help each other buy what their children needed. In other words, they organized themselves. Now they cultivate one field in common and have a person in charge and a treasurer.

The young people spoke in their turn. They said, "To get money we must go to the city." Then we reflected together, "Is this really the only way? What can we do right here?" Some young people started to sell peanuts so they could make a living while staying in the village. Women began to knit clothing and manufacture peanut oil. For us, the community means people who reflect together to see why their life is different and to find a new outlook.

There is no doubt that this experience gives hope to people who seek to live and have a future. In this particular village, the millet granary became the axis of church activity. During the long months of the dry season, communities and villages were unified around land, water and millet. All this helped people go beyond the usual dead-ends of development, which is nothing other than a destructive integration into the world market, creating a socio-political and economic situation where growing cotton for export benefits only the traditional leaders, the ranks of the administration, the dignitaries of the government party, and the multinational corporations.

This experience gives an insight into the potential force the Word of God can have when it is liberated from its yokes, as Vincent Cosmao says.[3] The poor have a way of backing us into a corner where we must make a choice, and then they use the Bible to show us that we must adopt a relevant pastoral program. They show us how disturbing the Word of God is—faced with injustices in villages and slums, excessive interest payments, arbitrary fines, detention without trial, forced labor in the fields of the chief, customary rents, the pulling-up of millet to grow cotton, and so on. In the face of all these problems, these efforts I describe are modest—not at all spectacular; but they are small steps toward living better.

Given the extent of corruption on all levels, it is very difficult to find a way out of our maze. Our countries are considered secure—a sort of fiscal paradise—for foreign investors. Soccer is the only subject one dares to discuss in total freedom. But within these new communities, people discover each other and the socio-economic conflicts that entrap them. People are speaking up and utilizing the energies of a heretofore paralyzed Africa. When these communities analyze their own difficulties, they discover the great anxieties of Africa today: growing inequities, the continuing deterioration of living conditions, and an increasing dependence on other countries.

Yet "representatives" of the people speak of a model of production that creates an élite who demand that peasants produce crops for export; and they do so in the name of development or the construction of a national economy. Overexploitation is being justified by ideological and patriotic arguments! Thus the strategy of the state and the strategy of the people collide—the peasant of northern Cameroon opposes the growing of cotton, and the peasant of Senegal opposes the peanut. The rural world finds itself struggling against the same structures of oppression, but now they are designed by the independent states rather than by the colonialists. Everywhere the basic features of the struggle are the same: growing export crops as opposed to diversified food crops, which base agriculture on the traditional techniques of peasant expertise—planting in cooperatives, rotation of crops, and adjustment to environmental conditions. The conflict is between an external orientation and nutritional self-reliance. The situation is the same through the Third World. In his book *Le sucre et la faim*, Robert Linhart shows us how Brazilian peasants of the northeast struggled against the new spread of sugar-cane imperialism and its ruthless requirements.[4] Likewise, black peasants in Africa wonder if they will be able to keep their lands to grow millet. They have collided with a model of development that pays little heed to growing crops for food.

An analysis in the heart of village communities of the causes of misery reveals the muted speech of the most exploited people in our society. Today basic communities liberate peasants to speak out in villages that have been pulled apart by the production of export crops, and whose authority has been replaced by the government's propaganda apparatus of radio, television, and the party press. Peasants who want to grow millet denounce this blind alley of development geared to outside interests as the prime cause of dependence and the cause of a series of inequities and misery. The current model of development is part of what can certainly be called a "vulgar ideology of development"—a plan that licenses whatever is used to starve a people, under the pretext of accumulating foreign exchange for the profit of a club of the affluent.

Popular Resistance and Creativity

While official and unofficial organs of the state continue to impose their model of development, the communities that we have been trying to form here and now insist that we also listen to what is *not* being said in official speeches in order to understand what is going on in the heart of the African bush. These new communities are identifying the cultural elements that would support a process of change, and they are looking for people who can motivate the villages. The communities are planning a form of development that keeps our actions and research today open to the alternative of a different future.

In this way, starting from the gospel, Africa is becoming reconciled with itself. Capital does not have to be king in all the areas where the single-crop economies of cocoa, peanuts, tea, or coffee have disrupted African agriculture. There are often isolated areas within the interior of countries where the people display their ability to resist and to be creative. Colonial history is peppered with stories of the suppression of peasant revolts. Historians tend to omit the stifled cries of an entire people who have been exploited repeatedly throughout centuries, in spite of the variations in the type of domination and in their resistance to it. Ever since the time African societies were first destructured by foreign trade, they have never stopped struggling to escape from its domination. This resistance is part of the memory of traditional Africa. But how can we draw on this source of popular knowledge and energy that has been neglected for so long, in order to devise and re-create conditions for survival today? This is the question presented to Africa today by the poor who are taking responsibility themselves and working in communities to change their living conditions.

We already have a rich base of reflection to help us rethink the problems of health care, education, famine, and dependence, and their real alternatives. As communities grasp the Word of God, they require the Christian churches to re-examine their practices of faith in dealing with problems that arise in the villages and slums. In the end, this "ministry of the granary" brings us back to a radical demand: that we live our faith in solidarity with the poor and the exploited in our societies.

The growth of inequalities of every sort, the degradation of the African peasantry, repression, dependence, including dependence on foreign interests, imperialism with all its legacies and its ideological apparatus challenge African Christians. Under the influence of our mother-churches, our faith has long been committed to a strategy of aid, based on a reading of Matthew 25:31-46 that emphasizes charity. Today we must move on to a strategy of liberation as we follow the crucified one of Golgotha who confronted everything that did not conform to God's plan. Today, as yesterday, we encounter the living God when and where God hears the cry of the poor and remembers the covenant. If we view the Eucharist itself as a sign of mutual exchange and as a political act, we must turn away from a world that prevents us from sharing. The Eucharist celebrates and anticipates that relationship of communion among human beings willed by God. It calls us to question radically all structures of injustice throughout the world.

A whole life is at stake as soon as we define faith in terms of a ministry that gets its hands dirty. Every manifestation of our faith today takes place in a world of domination and injustice. Can we remain untouched? Or must we live with our people? In what way? How can we feel ourselves genuinely involved in this situation? We can no longer think in terms of a commitment by those who call themselves pure—those people who have experienced a personal conversion and are now like foreigners, trying to convert others so as to lift them out of this sinful world.

Our faith can no longer be described simply and exclusively in terms of the Roman setting. Rome risks marginalizing the problems of the Third World because it is caught up in its preoccupations with what we may aptly call a three-dimensional universe centered on the doctrine of sin, the sacraments, and grace. The churches of the Third World have other concerns, other preoccupations, other objectives: to see their people free themselves from oppression, from slavery, poverty, and hunger.

This is the liberating commitment to our people that we celebrate in our communities. God transforms us while transforming the world, through the provocative power of the gospel. The heart of our faith is to discover in Christ that God who frees and transforms life in solidarity with human beings, and this must happen in a world where God speaks to us and summons us by the facts of injustice and by every situation of misery.

One thing is very clear to me: faith is at work among the poor in every place when we begin with our own cross, and are called to confess Jesus crucified. Remember the words of the leader Bouba: "It is our sufferings that Jesus bears, our sorrow that Jesus carries." These were his words after his entire village was forced to pull up their millet and plant cotton to increase the prosperity of the multinational corporations and the governing minorities.

The Cross of the Third World

If we view the cross of Jesus Christ as the cross of the Third World, the very existence of the Third World shows us what sin is and how it is structured in history. The Third World carries within itself the hidden Christ. It is the historic body of Jesus Christ today.

We must go and rediscover Christ in the slums, in places of misery and domination, among the majority of the poor and the oppressed people. It is the Third World that allows the church to make salvation in Jesus Christ visible. How do we say "I believe in God" in a community where Christians are organizing to resist a society structured in injustice and corruption? And this is the question asked of our faith today in most of the countries of our continent. Our choice is simple: either we choose to work with the agents of change to create a world habitable for all, or we choose not to work with them. If we choose to be agents of liberation, how do we talk about God?

In the modern West until now, it has seemed that any discussion in which God is the subject is socially insignificant. Theology continues to be practiced even though many people accept as an unavoidable cultural axiom that it is impossible to have any meaningful language dealing with God. Thus theology is in crisis in a world where atheism has somehow become a social necessity.[5] For some time, the Christianity of special devotions and confraternities has disincarnated the faith, leading from passivity to resignation in the face of misery and injustice. To speak of God afresh today, in a post-atheistic world, perhaps the church and theology should take up those questions coming from the periphery, from the margins.

What God do the people of the West believe in? What is the Good News for those who live in dominating societies? The answer is simple: "Join the front of resistance formed by all who are rising up against the forms of exploitation and domination!" As Nyerere pointed out, we are entering a time of challenge when the church must grasp the opportunity to identify itself with the poor of God. This is what is happening when we can no longer neglect those sectors of our societies where the question of food is a question of the relation of God to his people (Matt. 25:37).

Christians should consider the failure of decades of development to date, and design a model of life that leaves room in our daily work for whatever may create a different future. Otherwise we are setting aside our century and our historical role, and irrevocably contributing to the coming of death. Death is already appearing here and there in the turns of daily life, as it does wherever cotton drives away millet.

In the painful march of the peoples of the Third World toward the victory of life, perhaps Christians should remember that the God of Life has lifted up the poor and fed the hungry. Today that God calls us to struggle for justice and right. Then we shall be able to sing the Magnificat, not in Latin, but in deeds, wherever faith is lived among the poor. We shall be able to sing the Magnificat in the slums, in the villages, in the streets—wherever we are—because the truth of God is fully engaged both in the countries of hunger and in the dominating societies.

If we wish to put the Christianity of museums behind us and restore to the gospel all its relevance, we must recognize that the question of God is being presented to the churches whenever famine and oppression are incompatible with God's plan for humanity and the world.

How can we not hear the frightening words of an African writer? Cheikh Hamidou Kane writes in *Ambiguous Adventure*:

> For a long time God's worshippers ruled the world. Did they do it in accordance with God's law? I do not know. I have learned that in the country of the Whites, the revolt against poverty and misery is not distinguished from the revolt against God. They say that the movement is spreading, and that soon, in the world that same cry against poverty will drown out the voice of the muezzins. What must have been the misbehavior of those who believe in God if, at the end of their reign over the world, the name of God should arouse the resentment of the starving?[6]

To believe today is a matter of faithfulness to the God of hope, who went out from himself to place himself at the side of human beings as they struggle to stand up erect in the image of the Risen One. Such a faith requires a fresh re-reading of revelation.

Notes

1. Anselme Tatianma Sanon, "Dimensions anthropologiques de l'Euchariste," in *La Documentation Catholique* 78 (19 July 1981): 721-728.

2. René Dumont, *False Start in Africa* (New York: Praeger, 1966). Translated by André Deutsch Ltd. from *L'Afrique noire est mal partie* (Paris, Seuil, 1962).

3. Vincent Cosmao, *Changing the World* (Maryknoll, NY: Orbis, 1984). Translated by John Drury from *Changer le monde: Une tâche pour l'Église* (Paris: Cerf, 1984).

4. Robert Linhart, *Le sucre et la faim: enquête dans les régions sucrières du Nord-Est Brésilien* (Paris: Éditions de Minuit, 1980).

5. Claude Geffre, "Non-Metaphysical Theology" in *A New Age in Theology* (New York: Paulist, 1974). Translated by Robert Shillenn, Francis McDonagh and Theodore L. Westow from *Un nouvel âge de la théologie* (Paris: Cerf, 1972).

6. Cheikh Hamidou Kane, *Ambiguous Adventure* (London: Heinemann, 1972; NY: Walker & Co., 1963), p. 11. Translated by Katherine Woods from *L'Aventure ambiguë* (Paris: Julliard, 1961).

Chapter 7

Is God Neutral?

There should be no further need to justify the urgency of rereading the gospel. It is difficult, though, for Christian churches to realize to what extent the face of God has been obscured over many long centuries. But since the beginning of the slave trade, what God has Christianity been talking about? This fundamental question plagues any understanding of faith by black people. The darkest periods of black African history corresponded generally to the times when access to God's truth was blocked by everything that tramples and disfigures humanity. Whenever fatalism triumphs and all the mechanisms of poverty and oppression shut the door on hope, God is on trial.

This has been happening in Africa for almost three hundred years. We Africans have been introduced to the Christian God by means of a theology of suffering, which seems to have been created so black people would learn to accept their historical status as a conquered people. That is the message of the curse on Canaan (Gen. 9:25)—a myth used in catechisms, preaching, and prayers to record the genesis of an entire people caught up in a tragedy of identity with outcasts. Yet the true face of God emerges from these shadows. It begins to take form as prisons are opened. As the heavy chains of oppression fall from the hands of captives, they raise their heads toward the God who takes their side. For me, this is the logic of the God of our faith.

The center of revelation is that a commitment has been made to the poor, and this commitment is rooted in a history where messianic dynamics are coming to life. The hope of the people will germinate from the tension between oppression and liberation that makes up the axis of revelation. The central core of biblical faith is the certainty that God encountered a people at a moment in its history—namely, at the time of the exodus from Egypt (Exod. 6:6-8). Israel's act of faith in God is revealed in his giving birth to a people freed from slavery and oppression (Deut. 26:1-11). This decisive intervention of God should not be forgotten by anyone throughout the generations (Deut. 8:11-19). Israel's confession of faith is the proclamation of God's liberating action in a foundational event that will continue to nourish and develop the people's memory. Believing means clinging to Yahweh as the only God to whom Israel owes its existence and dignity. Thus, the remembrance of the exodus from Egypt remains the center of faith and worship.

Today, through acts, symbols, liturgical gatherings, prayer, and festivals, we must reactivate the experience of that God who brings humanity out of servitude into freedom and service (Deut. 11:2-4). And as the remembrance of this basic experience engenders hope in believers, they must constantly go beyond the past and open themselves to the future (Isa. 43:18-19). The "locus" in which God is experienced lies in the promise of a liberation continually renewed (Isa. 61:1-2, 10:11; Bar. 5). Throughout the whole of scripture, which can be seen as a rereading of the exodus, God brings forth words and deeds, revealing a God who is the last refuge of his beloved people subjected to exploitation, violence, and misery. God's total commitment is to those people with no defense—"To oppress the poor is to insult their creator" (Prov. 14:31). Because the Lord freed a small oppressed people from slavery, concern for the "little ones," the slaves and strangers, should mark all our experiences and social relationships. The commandments witness to this God of deliverance: "You must not molest or oppress the stranger, for you lived as strangers in the land of Egypt" (Exod. 22:20).

To understand the preaching of the prophets, we must enter into the whole experience of faith that underlies the Old Testament. When the prophets denounce the injustices of their own time, with a violence that may surprise us, they are simply taking up the cause of the disinherited in the name of God. Exploitation and corruption demand that people speak out (Amos 8:4-8). How are we to remain indifferent in a world of plunder and violence where assassination is the way to power (Zeph. 1:13)?

Every form of brutality must be rejected (Jer. 9:1-8), along with the amassing and concentration of wealth that causes others to starve (Ps. 14:4, 53:4) and dispossesses many (Isa. 5:8; Mic. 2:2 ff.). Amos accuses the ruling classes of piling up wealth in their palaces by violence and oppression (Amos 3:10). Jeremiah condemns King Jehoiakim for having exploited the labor of fellow citizens by making them "work for nothing without paying them wages" in order to obtain for himself "an imposing palace with spacious rooms upstairs, . . . paneled it with cedar and painted it vermillion" (Jer. 22:13-14). In a society where the rich wallow in luxury at the expense of the exploited and participate in raucous festivals (Amos 6:1-6), the prophets recall that there can be no true worship without justice (Amos 4:4 ff., 5:21-24; Hosea 6:6). Injustice to the poor is a real crime (Ec. 34:25-27; Ps. 10:8-10, 64:4). Faithfulness to the God of the covenant implies human rights and justice (Ps. 140:13, 10:17-18). Thus, freeing "the despoiled from those who despoil them" (Jer. 30:16) is a religious act that corresponds to the will of God. This is the true fast of which Isaiah speaks (58:6-9). No longer may the poor be sold for a pair of sandals (Amos 2:6, 8:6). In a place where rulers crush the weak (Amos 5:11; Neh. 5:1-5), the prophet must take up a ministry of watchfulness (Ezek. 33:1-9). God is too fully involved in struggles for justice to remain deaf to the cry of the unfortunate (Ps. 86:1, 22:24). In the tribulations of world politics, Israel must not look forward to the execution of any plan other than God's (Isa. 14:26).

The most basic feature of our biblical heritage, therefore, is attentiveness to those who live in a state of oppression and suffering under unjust social structures. The God of the Bible is revealed in the midst of every type of slavery. God sends witnesses to stand in solidarity with these people and to work for their liberation. God remains constantly preoccupied with those who are mistreated by other humans. Because of God's overwhelming preoccupation with the poor, the task of the Messiah will be to free the poor who call for help (Ps. 72:12-14). The hoped-for arrival of the Messiah nourishes the expectation of the people. *God is not neutral.* God is revealed as the one who brings justice to the oppressed (Ps. 146:7-9).

Finally, Jesus of Nazareth comes to reveal the true name of the

God of the exodus (John 17:6, 8:28, 13:19; Exod. 3:14). The incarnation is the supreme event of our faith—God's final word to us (John 1:14; Heb. 1:1-2). It is difficult to realize its full significance unless we grasp it through the world of poverty and oppression. The real world of the gospel is one of hunger, wealth and injustice, sickness, rejection, slavery, and death. It is precisely through the structures of such a world that God is revealed. God is present through Jesus of Nazareth, who, in the incarnation, reveals God's omnipotence in weakness and establishes a form of conspiracy between God and the downtrodden.

The Gospel at the Heart of the Conflict

God's revelation through the incarnation obliges us to unmask the ultimate scandal of our faith: Jesus Christ made a radical choice in favor of those considered to be the dregs of the world. For a long time, this reality has been covered up by the dominant theology we have inherited down through the centuries. The dominant theology is a theology of the rich. It has always justified and tried to legitimize those ecclesiastical practices in which it is rooted. The church has domesticated the gospel by subordinating its message to the interests of the powerful. We shouldn't be surprised that it has neglected to question the privileges of the rich in the name of the subversive practice of the historical Jesus.

In spite of dogmatic affirmations about the realism of the incarnation ("true man"), the dominant theology tends to spiritualize Christ to the point that we forget that he took on human reality with all its tensions and conflicts. In the words of the French Canadian biblical scholar André Myre:

> We don't understand Jesus if we make of him a mild man who loved equally all those he met without exception. Jesus is a man who made choices, because he had fully received the intuitive knowledge that God is the God of the poor; he saw that he had to translate this essential characteristic of God into active solidarity with the world's unprivileged. . . . In his choices, he clearly witnesses that God is with the poor. . . . Instead of marching up front with the powerful, rich, and educated, God takes a place at the end of the column, as

history marches on, and "wastes" his time with those who
drag their feet in the rear.[1]

From the heart of his radically and uniquely close experience of
God (John 1:18, 14:9, 17:23), Jesus announces the good news,
starting with an option for the poor. He enters a world divided
between rich and poor, masters and slaves, educated and unedu-
cated, Gentiles and Jews. Deliberately, he takes his place among the
poor and exploited. He says "Happy are the poor" and "Alas to
you who are rich" or who "tie up heavy burdens, and lay them on
peoples' shoulders, but will not lift a finger to move them" (Matt.
23:4). In a characteristic style, Jesus' parable of Lazarus and the
rich man (Luke 16) recaptures this startling and provocative contrast. The story is so harsh that a certain well-known pastoral letter
found it appropriate to soften and moralize it, correcting the gospel
to speak of a "good" Lazarus and the "wicked" rich man. Jesus
tells the rich man that sharing is a requirement of the Kingdom, in
line with the teaching of the covenant and the prophets (Luke
16:29). The actions of Jesus are rooted in the prophetic tradition of
protest against oppression and injustice, and rise far beyond all
comfortable and acceptable values. They take their dynamism
from an experience of the God who destroys idols,[2] and they are
marked, above all, by their nonconformity. Emphasizing this basic
characteristic of the gospel is a duty for Christians today.

The center of Jesus' preaching and acting is a Kingdom of God
for the sake of the poor. For it is important to remember that
Christianity begins with a criticism of religion, which is, at the same
time, a criticism of all of society, of human relationships and of
power (Matt. 20:25). He who "had come forth from God" (John
13:3) never focuses his ministry on the rites or sacrifices of the
temple; rather, he announces their radical insufficiency in the
fourth gospel in a form of cultic anti-judaism (John 2:19-22; 4:21-
24). Jesus did not feel himself called to restore the dignity of Israel
by leading people to receive a baptism of repentance in the waters
of the Jordan, as did John the Baptist. He decided to do something
different.

The background of Jesus' activity was his refusal to sanctify the
system of cleanness and uncleanness that regulated the conduct of
daily life (Mark 7:14; Matt: 15:11-20). This system gave preference

to ritual concerns, and downplayed any struggle to establish justice for the poor and to end exploitation (Lev. 25:14-18; Deut. 15:1-18). Prevailing religious practices were characterized by an ideology of uncleanness (Lev. 11-16; Mark 7:2-7) and the centralization of temple worship, which led to a veritable exploitation of popular piety (John 2:13-18). In speaking out against these practices, Jesus affirmed the possibility of suppressing injustice and restoring fraternal communion.

Such criticism of an existing religious system inspires attitudes and behavior that scandalize people and disrupt a whole social order. Jesus, a Jew, will speak with a Samaritan woman beside a well (John 4:9). We will see him include Philip, an unclean Greek, among his intimates. He is seen drawing close to those who have been shunned by pious believers. By eating with "tax collectors and sinners," he upsets the righteous and the specialists in God's ways (Matt. 9:9-12). His parables and actions illustrate a practice that confounds existing relationships as it transforms them. A good example is the healing of the leper (Mark 1:40-41), an action that questions a model of society that legalizes exclusion through the system of cleanness and uncleanness (Lev. 13:9).

But the real issue throughout the gospels is the oppressive laws, which assure the prosperity of some at the cost of excluding others. The healing of the man with the withered hand (Mark 3:1 ff.) and the incident of the ears of corn picked on the sabbath (Mark 2:23-38) serve to free people from laws that can reduce people to slavery in order to maintain the *status quo*. The symbolic action of sharing bread reveals the God of the hungry (Luke 1:53; Mark 6:30-43) and questions a social system based on accumulation and dispossession.

In the end, the gospel confronts a strategy of domination leading to hunger, set in a world structure where the administration of the wealth of the earth is monopolized by those who control the economic and political apparatus. Jesus reveals God and his option for the poor and the little ones—in the heart of a society built for ideological and religious reasons on the basis of marginalization, misery, and oppression.

Jesus' experience of relationship with the Father (John 8:21-30; 10:30; 20:17; 13:3) is inseparable from the practice by which Jesus turns toward the rabble who have been rejected by the teachers of the law and the priests of the temple (John 8:1-12). He does not hold himself at an equal distance from the two groups engaged in struggle—the rich and the poor, the exploiters and the exploited. By his life and his action, he constantly takes the side of the poor, the humiliated, and the defenseless, against the rich, the pious, and the powerful. He does not hate the rich, but he will not tolerate the exploitation or slavery of men and women. He came, as he says himself, to free the oppressed (Luke 4:17-21).

The Sermon on the Mount, which constitutes the central message of the New Testament, is a message of hope (Luke 6:20-23). It cannot be reduced to a catechism for those people who search for perfection. Because the Beatitudes describe concrete situations of suffering, they remind us that the Kingdom of God cannot fail to be a kingdom of justice that will benefit all the disinherited of the earth, and all persons who are burdened or humiliated by the misery that makes them incapable of helping themselves. If the Kingdom of God also means the liberation of the oppressed, the good news for the poor is that the God of Jesus Christ is the defender of those who cannot defend themselves. The source of the conflict that leads Jesus to death is the deliberate refusal of some to believe that when Jesus identifies himself with the poor and the little ones (Matt. 25), he is revealing the Father and attesting that the good news is that God wants people to live (Mark 2:23-27; John 10:10).

Viewing the World from the Cross

Jesus' death cannot be separated either from his life that precedes and illuminates it, or from his resurrection that gives it meaning. It is not a question of magic, but of the basic human reality taken on by Jesus through a life of radical faithfulness to his mission. His death is the consummation of that mission. His life of solidarity with the poor and rejected is the key to a credible interpretation of his death in the context of our life today. The death of Jesus is the inevitable dénouement of a drama linked to the whole story of his life—an unending struggle against oppressive socioreligious forces and structures. A victim of repressive violence, Jesus pays for the boldness of his subversive ideas with his life.

The gospel is the written account of a praxis that caused division among those people who based their lives on the Old Testament. Even today, the death of Jesus must be understood as a situation in which the presence of God is perceived through actions that break away from the dominant religion and society. Jesus dies at Jerusalem, which is the center of political and religious power where the symbolic order of cleanness and uncleanness is institutionalized by worship in the temple. Jesus confronts the dominant system in its own fiefdom. The cross, which cries out God's love for humanity, incarnates Jesus' plan to bring the good news to the poor and oppressed. Jesus is the prophet who brings a new meaning to the reading of the Bible—a reading that serves and liberates humanity in a society that favors the worship and observation of the law to the detriment of life and justice. Jesus' death is the result of his option for the poor and oppressed. The contemporary society, in turn, condemns Jesus as a blasphemer for having shown the God of the exodus to the poor.

The death of the Lord, which is central to the church's experience and faith, reflects conflicts throughout history where God has always been on the side of the weak. The crucified Jesus takes upon himself the cries of everyone, from Abel (Gen. 4:8) to the worker deprived of his wages (James 5:4). Jesus died so that people can stand upright—that is the center of the gospel message. To live out that radical message in its fullness, we must never hide the concrete conflicts within existence and society. To "follow Jesus" is to live out his subversive plan, his stance for the poor against situations of misery and oppression. The presence of misery and oppression is a basic form of the "sin of the world" that contradicts the kingdom of justice and freedom inaugurated by Jesus of Nazareth. Jesus tranforms the cross from an instrument of humiliation into an instrument of struggle against slavery and death. For Christians and the church, the liberation of the poor, then, is the basic issue at stake in the death of Jesus. Christians must place themselves beside Jesus for the life of the world. The execution of Jesus, with all its gravity of suffering and death, asks us to decide whether we are in fact in solidarity with those who struggle against the forces of death at work in history.

It is true that the crucifixion is not the culmination of Jesus' life or of our faith (1 Cor. 15:3-14). It is the resurrection of Jesus that is the summit of revelation. This central event of the history of salvation fulfills the promise made to the people of God: "We have come here to tell you the Good News. It was to our ancestors that God made the promise but it is to us, their children, that he has fulfilled it. He raised up Jesus." (Acts 13:32-33). In resurrecting the dead once and for all, Jesus proclaims victory over the forces of death and inaugurates a new world. But how can we celebrate the resurrection where millions of men and women live in suffering and oppression? How can the resurrection of Jesus become an historical experience in the struggle for life itself by those who are weak and without power? How does the resurrection of the humiliated begin today?

All these questions lead us to the heart of the Bible and of our faith. We know that Jesus re-read all of revelation in the light of the Easter event, "starting with Moses and going through all the prophets" (Luke 24:27, 44). There can be no understanding of scripture without the resurrection. As Africans, how can we live and proclaim the Easter message today when we are already living out the passion of Jesus in history? If the poor and oppressed are the presence of the crucified God, can we read the Bible apart from contemporary situations of poverty and oppression? A new reading of scripture is already underway by the church in every place where peasants are reduced to pariahs, and in every hovel where another calvary looms. We must question everything we have learned about the meaning of Jesus' death and about faith in his resurrection—whether from catechisms, theological instruction, devotions, or piety. In the end, does this heritage of catechetics and pietism have any real meaning at all today? Too often, the church still seems to speak from another world, a world that does not represent the daily life of the poor and oppressed. Yet the redemptive cross not only implies an overall critique of a world opposed to God's plan; it also calls for a boundless reservoir of energy for criticism and for change to be used in every basic human situation. Nothing should be exempt from change.

When we look at the world from the cross, we discover that what we are living does not yet correspond to God's definitive promise and its full realization. Any reference to the cross implies that we are searching in history for what comes closest to the world willed by God. The fullness of life for the poor must be included in any true confession of Jesus crucified. If the will of God is to be carried out through a new genesis of humanity and the world, the cross implies the incarnation of the Word in the suffering of our peoples and the involvement of God in the process of liberation. Salvation, which is life in its fullness, then presupposes that we Africans take responsibility for our present and our future.

From this perspective we can see that taking responsibility in the historical drama of salvation belongs to our experience of faith. Living in the universe of the cross and of the resurrection implies one radical peculiarity: a state of affairs can change. The reign of death can be reversed. Because Jesus lived the passion of the people through his own passion, he will never be found hovering on the edge of the efforts and struggles of the people who today appear as the suffering servants. Jesus entered into the world of suffering. We know today that the suffering of people is not natural; it does not result from any human limitations. Instead, it is produced by people, by groups in power, and by models of society and culture. Insofar as Jesus saw the presage of his coming passion in the poor, the oppressed, and the marginalized, the resurrection is real and complete only when the poor pass from death to life.

In the end, what are the contemporary historical and social conditions that actually produce the message whenever the church reads holy scripture and proclaims Jesus Christ? Is "theo-logy" (talk about God) involved in the daily drama of the poor and exploited? Is the message meaningful to listeners in the same way as the message of Jesus was? Remember that Jesus took on the culture of the people and spoke the language of peasants and shepherds to make his words meaningful. Doesn't "theo-logy" actually fail to speak about the God of the poor by shutting itself up in a universe of the culture of the rich and powerful?

It is disturbing to see that the gospel has been used to justify oppressive powers. But an imperial image of Christ did play a large role in the history of colonial conquests, in the massacre of American Indians, and in the slave trade. In the last century, Christian missions themselves were an initiative carried out by a Christianity well integrated into the expansion of the West throughout the world. It seems that the gospel has been used in this way to alienate. Historically, it has been unusual if a revolution did not begin by criticizing religion and the church. Indeed, most Christians admit to an "ideological slowness"; they hesitate to take up the important issues that mobilize groups to become social agents involved in the process of change.

All of this should lead us to reflection. Throughout history, violence has been done to the gospel in the practice of faith. The resulting question may seem brutal: How can we "liberate" the gospel so that it can become the leaven of liberation in a socio-religious context where we discover that the God of Jesus Christ refuses to accept the role the church has assigned to him, by sanctifying powers which, in fact, he opposes. What "theo-logy" underlies our experience of God today? How can we prevent the cry of freedom of the people from becoming a cry of freedom from God and the church—as has happened before in Western history? In other words, how can we escape from a "theo-logy" that forces our faith and the church to play conservative roles, wherein preachers, catechists, spiritual advisers and pastors impose on God a repressive function incompatible with Jesus' evangelical plan?

In Africa we have reached a turning point in Christian life and thought. We must resolve not to turn God into an alienating idol. In order to discover once again the power of the Christian message to criticize and change the order of things, we must abandon all the catechisms and sermons that do no more for us than anesthetize our people.

Notes

1. A. Myre, *Cri de Dieu, espoir des pauvres* (Montréal: Éditions Paulines, 1977), p. 9.

2. C. Duquoc, *Dieu différent* (Paris: Cerf, 1977).

Part III

Christianity Faces
the Challenges of Africa

Chapter 8

The Gospel Is at the Heart
of Conflicts

African Christians need to discover that they have been given a unique observation post and, consequently, have good reason to be "lookouts." "The lookout shouts, 'On a watchtower, Lord, I stand all day; and at my post I keep guard all night' " (Isa. 21:8). The people cry, "Watchman, what time of night?" and the watchman answers, "The morning is coming, then night again" (Isa. 21:11-12). Jesus urges us to learn to read the signs of the times (Matt. 16:1-4) so that we can interpret our period of history in harmony with the grace of our time.

The Basic Conflict between Rich and Poor

Jerusalem did not recognize the time of its visitation: "Your house will be left to you desolate" (Matt. 23:39). To escape from this sad fate, we need to discern what innovations our age is bringing to the Christian faith. That is the basis on which we can build the future. If we do not challenge beliefs and practices established in another place for another time, we risk overlooking the specific grace of the present. Nowadays, when the majority of Christians are no longer in the West but in the Third World, isn't it time for us Africans to reclaim the gospel, and bring our disinherited peoples face to face with it? For, in the words of Paul VI, we face critical situations where "bold transformations" and "urgent reforms should be undertaken without delay."[1]

115

Christianity has endured for a long time, maintaining its Graeco-Latin heritage within the context of a society fashioned by Western models. Today the church must examine that entire experience, recognizing that it has lost its cultural monopoly as well as the theological systems that seemed to guarantee it. A new age is beginning that gives great importance to non-Western churches, and Africa plays a decisive role in this migration of the church to the southern hemisphere. While the loss of China has been felt as a heavy blow to the history of missions, Paul VI did not hesitate to declare that Africa is "the new homeland of Christ."

The center of gravity of Christianity continues to shift. It is possible that the black continent will become a real prize for the church. The one hundred and fifty million Christians in Africa today are a significant resource on the religious map of the world and for the vitality of the Christian faith. But the Christian communities of Africa can truly set free their dynamism only if the church agrees to stop standardizing and centralizing its practices and rules. The paths of the future are found on the equator and in the tropics where a majority of Christians now live. If the church accepts the displacement brought about by the emergence of the peoples of the Third World, it must destroy its center of power for the sake of its outermost reaches. Nothing can justify, then, that African Christians should be at best barely tolerated within the church, for we bear important questions for the Christian church of our time. It is possible that our questions are the best way for God to speak to the people of today.

Starting with the meeting of non-aligned nations in Bandung, Indonesia, in 1955, peoples who had been excluded too long from history irrupted, and upset the basic assumptions of the contemporary world. The years since decolonization in black Africa have given many people nothing more than a flag to wave and an obligation to join a single political party. Today's basic conflict, which divides and sets at odds the poor of the African Third World and the global system of hegemony, remains a daily reality that Christians cannot ignore. In several declarations devoted to legitimate differences in the expression of the Christian faith, the church has certainly begun to respond to concerns for traditions and cultures long forgotten or misunderstood. African religions are finally emerging from the illusions of belief and exotic stereotypes in which triumphant colonialism had entrapped them.

But to what degree is the African church itself alert to the awakening of the poor and oppressed classes who have been smothered by the apparatus of neocolonial domination? There is a danger that African Christians may continue to live in a world defined by the East-West conflict, even though the true conflict of our time is between North and South. In reality, the North-South conflict reveals the struggle of the poor on behalf of the life and the future of all humanity. Millions of people are affirming that they are alive and that they do not wish to die. Their choice raises serious questions about all the models of society and development that have been designed to destroy life.

How can we accept that millions of dollars are spent each year on armaments while the majority of the inhabitants of the planet lack jobs, food, shelter, health care, and education? This basic question relegates the East-West conflict to a wholly secondary and relative position. The arsenals of weapons in Africa—mostly paid for with peasant labor—incarnate the "anti-granary." In view of the prevalence of famine, Christians and the churches must face the question of how we can prevent our countries from being turned into weapon-markets for the prosperity and triumph of a system of death that does not hesitate to corrupt itself to support unpopular (but profitable) régimes. How can we witness to the Lord of Life in a world where the traffickers of death reign supreme? We must deal with this question in our experience of faith, entering into the basic conflict between rich and poor.

We must return to daily life in Africa where the conflict between rich and poor is manifested in the relationships of power being formed among the different emerging levels of society. No part of the African reality suggests a homogeneous, unchanging world where people live in perfect accord and are sheltered from any tensions or conflicts that might disrupt a socio-economic and cultural equilibrium. Research, novels, plays, and films all point to cultural conflicts born from a brutal collision between Africa and the colonial world. These conflicts particularly affect the younger generations, who are torn between an old culture that they reject, often without knowing anything about it, and a new culture to which they aspire, without the means to achieve it. It is difficult to comprehend the tensions that arise within families when the young fail to make themselves understood; yet the young have clearly separated themselves from the adults by their desire to get rid of the same traditions that their elders are trying to preserve. Even deeper rips in the social fabric are likely to pass unnoticed in régimes where a desire for consensus tends to hide the ever-growing contradictions between the state and the people. These régimes proletarianize the people in the countryside, and doom them to misery in an economic order that condemns whole peoples to dispossession and dependence. Africans need support today as accomplished strategists speculate in food shortages and imprison millions of men and women in "the gulag of hunger."[2]

The people who benefit from African famine are not all overseas, working at high levels where all-powerful states parcel out the resources of the planet among themselves, and rearrange relationships among peoples to benefit their own economies and interests. The real Africa cannot be seen in the distorting prism of the "equality" of misery. The real Africa is seen only through the economic and social disparities that result as new African élites are integrated into the dominant world system. While peasants are abandoned to their fate, the ruling groups prosper from their alliances with external economic powers. The ideology of national unity, worked out by the middle classes that emerged from the colonialized societies, masks the class nature of the African postcolonial states. Hence, any talk of opposition or conflict between the state and the people disturbs the harmony of official dogma. Hiding growing economic inequities is an on-going self-appointed task of the élites who promote various forms of an ideology of consensus.

We must adopt methods of analysis that disturb the privileges people acquire under the protection of cadres who, in turn, live in the shadow of power. A definitive analysis is the only way to get a clear picture of the reality, which is continuously masked by official reports, and reinforced by myths disseminated in tourist leaflets directed at societies with an itch for the exotic. Those who lead people to believe that Africans live in a world without conflicts fall back on ideology and ignore reality. The reality is that the "little people" know they are being marginalized by the "children of the whites" who tend to confiscate the fruits of developmental projects and administer national resources for their own profit.[3] African Christians must redefine their identity and their mission, starting with this basic conflict between the base and the summit of society that internalizes and reveals the North-South conflict.

What is at stake here is the role of the gospel in the great market-place of religion, at a time when Christian institutions transplanted from overseas demonstrate their lack of power against the prolifer-ation of sects invading Africa. The church must ask itself if the Christian faith is relevant in a time of social crisis when "Africans are throwing themselves desperately into mystical movements and organizations brought in from overseas."[4] The phenomenon of sects coincides with worsening living conditions, caused by the failure of the models of development promoted by the ruling classes to build a "society for all." All evidence indicates that the misery of people in search of security is a fertile ground that leads to the reactivation of ancestral religious traditions and the deploy-ment of new spiritual movements. This can be observed in many countries through the degradation of "the sectors of life where people are particularly ill-treated."[5]

> Entrapped and desperate, people often succumb to the prose-lytism of sects and freemasonry. . . . In their disarray, those in quest of salvation become an easy prey for propagandists, whose promises sound the more alluring and fascinating, the deeper the internal distress of their victims.[6]

In taking up this challenge, pastors and theologians rightly insist on the need to root the Christian faith in our African cultural world in order to respond to the malaise and frustration of many Chris-tians on the twin levels of culture and religion.[7] But if the search for an African Christianity is to reach Africans in the unity of their soul and body, it must be based in the concreteness of life where the violence of misery is as fatal as any form of cultural alienation. We are living in a "situation of apocalypse" in Africa where "we can no longer keep silent."[8] A faith lived at ground level is perhaps the only adequate response demanded by millions of young people living in the streets, without jobs or food, exposed to the brutality of misery and poverty. While masses of the poor are flocking to sects, bars, drugs, or prostitution to escape the mechanisms of hunger and unemployment, faithfulness to the gospel requires us to work for a Christianity which is credible to them.

A Time for Change

Sensitive topics that raise questions of conscience for us religious leaders, though, will not present equal difficulties to men and women whose basic rights are ignored—access to drinking water, a balanced diet, adequate health care, jobs, education. What the churches ordinarily talk about is the deliberate choice of clergy who are aware of their responsibility to decide what is to be believed, to be thought, and to be done. As a result, these clergy set aside questions, situations, needs, and hopes of people and groups whose role in the church is limited to receiving and carrying out what has been decided from above. An examination of the priorities and major themes of church practice shows this to be true. Church discussions rarely refer to what actually happens in the heart of villages and slums in order to determine the basic outlines of the church's practices, which, after all, did originate in a concrete situation where God intervened on behalf of humanity. We know, for example, that problems of marriage, family, reconciliation, and penance are subjects of great importance in the life of Christian communities. But it is dismaying to discover that answers already exist to all these questions; they have been decided by the church hierarchy. Thus it appears that the actual practice of the churches is limited to reproducing models that have never been reexamined within the specific African contexts. These contexts now demand that we reevaluate the essentials of our faith.

When their profound questions and specific challenges are marginalized or ignored, Africans are tempted to turn elsewhere, to where someone will consider their actual conditions, questions, and anxieties. Thus the appeal of the sects today lies in the deception experienced by men and women who now refuse to be identified with the Christian faith as it is being preached and lived in the churches implanted in Africa. Can the church reconcile itself with the new generations who are joining the sects, if it willingly takes on our African identity, but excludes its socio-economic and political dimensions? The question must be asked.

African cultural patrimony is a real challenge to our Christian faith. To go beyond believing "by proxy" has been the great hope obsessing African Christians for a quarter of a century. But to be complete and total—to be credible—requires that the Christian faith in Africa identify with the anxieties and hopes of the "'little" people of the villages, slums, and hills. We cannot find free expression in our churches without acknowledging the tragedy of the hungry within the richness of our continent, and the condition of those people excluded by our societies. We need, then, to review our practices and options, our research, and our attitudes in order to overcome the separation between our desire to emancipate a church still under tutelage, and our hope for liberation, which motivates the African. What meaning can there be to the faith of local churches that seek to liberate themselves from insupportable yokes, if they don't participate as well in the struggles of peasants or herdsmen who also carry heavy yokes?

A Break Is Needed

There seems to be a need for a break in the African churches—a need to stop a certain number of activities, for a long time if necessary. We risk becoming too involved in these activities today; instead, we need to rethink our faith in light of the great challenges of today's Africa. This sabbatical experience would help the churches understand that they cannot satisfy themselves by criticizing and threatening others, by arousing or exhorting, without looking at themselves at the same time and questioning what they are about. If they truly follow the gospel, which is not an alibi for Christians but a call to conversion and the leaven for liberation, they will have to stop speaking of truth from the heights of pulpits, and submit to self-criticism. They will have to unmask their lack of family spirit and their lack of solidarity with people and movements who struggle to break the unjust chains of poverty and oppression.

Troubling situations demand attention. While the indigenization of Christianity is the theme of many declarations, studies, and speeches, the concrete conditions of the people who carry the African culture are not really an object of major concern. In certain churches, young rural people are not even able to find a national chaplain to guide their movement. That may seem surprising in African countries where agriculture is the foundation of the economy. But while the bishops are obsessed with the formation of clergy, they do not see that the concerns of the peasants play a role in their search for a priestly model that fits into rural communities.

In the cities, where school systems inherited from colonialism tend to separate urban youth from their families, there is no indication that the churches are channelling their resources into popular education, although they are doing so for their seminaries. But we know that the young people who form the majority of the population encounter major problems with education, unemployment, health care, food, and housing—all of which affect their future. There is reason to ask whether the churches have not chosen to become churches for old women and children. Christianity is in danger of being considered obsolete. As long as church buildings are filled and yet no questions are asked about the commitment of Christians to social problems, the decision-making groups, which influence the future by their plans for social development projects, will remain beyond the influence of the church.

Equally serious is the attitude of the churches that leads them to give way before forces of oppression. Here and there, of course, voices are starting to be heard denouncing unfairness and injustice.[9] But these verbal positions coexist with practices that actually resist any efforts at renewal or research growing from instances of injustice. We still pay allegiance to foreign church implantations that do not allow themselves to be questioned about the basic confrontation between rich and poor. This is true throughout all of Africa. Christians are still subject to models that administer religious affairs using patterns inherited from older forms of Christianity. As Albert Nolan has explained:

> The basic reason why we are in crisis is the model we are still working with, especially among grassroot people in the parish. This model may be defined as *sacramental consumption*. The church is a kind of agency that provides the people with sacraments and other ritual services. . . . These products or services are regarded as necessary in order for people to obtain the salvation or health of their souls. . . . The church is this supermarket of the spiritual or sacramental. Following this model, a parish and those responsible for its ministry try to sell their goods to as many people as possible for the health of their souls. That means that they try to find the largest

number of people with the minimal number of needs and demands. . . .

We should not be surprised then if a pastoral letter or encyclical on social justice is read in a parish and produces no effect. Since the faithful see the church only according to this model, they decide the letter is irrelevant and without meaning, an intervention of the church in questions of a political nature. . . . Fewer and fewer people feel the necessity to save their souls or to make use of the services of the church. Those who want something else, such as justice, liberation, or peace, look elsewhere. The root of the problem is the need to change this type of church. . . .

We need to turn to the type of churches described so well in "*Evangelii nuntiandi*"—a church concerned, above all, with the salvation and total liberation of the person, of society, and of the material universe.[10]

The Christians of Africa are searching for a church that will rediscover its evangelical identity by determining to stand beside the multitudes who seek to escape from all forms of marginalization. The tasks of the Kingdom of God require us to abandon all church models and practices that do not include incarnation of the faith in our condition of the poor and exploited. A break in church activities will allow this option—if we decide not to jeopardize the future of African Christianity for many centuries. We must have the courage to leave our areas of security, to step out of our religious ghettos, and to encounter the generations whose hopes have been betrayed today by the magnitude of inequities and by all the forces of oppression.

The Calvary of a People

In black Africa, where abortive declarations of independence still arouse bitter disillusions, daily life is a long calvary that raises questions for disciples of the crucified Jesus. Little by little the African churches are coming to realize this. The bishops of Zaire recently asked: "How long must we wait for a little happiness?" They continued, "Fulfillment is constantly postponed. And while we wait—shameless exploitation, organized plundering for the profit of foreigners and their successors, while the largest part of the people stagnate in misery, in conditions often artificially created."[11] Few countries escape this basic situation. Meeting in Nairobi in 1978, the Symposium of Episcopal Conferences of Africa and Madagascar (SECAM) noted that a process of recolonization is going on all across the continent. In order to live our faith in the world of today, we must take measure of the burdens of domination that paralyze Africa. Meeting in Yaoundé in 1981, the African bishops invited us:

> . . . to become aware of international domination from a political, economic, social, cultural point of view . . . to realize the control of the multinational corporations. . . . All these forces burden the African continent; they perpetuate unjust situations and create often insurmountable obstacles on the road to development and to economic and social progress.[12]

It is impossible to have a naive vision of our people's reality today. While the effects of dependency continue to be generated, and all the forms of domination are renewed, our destiny cannot be attributed to any curse or fatality. On the contrary, as John Paul II said on his first trip to Africa in 1980, "There are still situations and systems within individual countries and in the relationships between states that are 'marked by injustice and social injury,' and that still condemn many people to hunger, disease, unemployment, lack of education, and stagnation in their process of development."[13] It is true that Africa is not just a playing-field for the great powers. We must be aware of the responsibility of the African ruling classes for the ongoing impoverishment of the masses. Injustice and oppression are generated from outside, but a train of miseries also results from the relationships between the African states and their people. The benefits of programs of modernization and efforts at growth are coopted by the élites in power.[14]

We must also consider the tragedy of families crushed by the rising costs of education, and of medical care in a health system that profits from illness. We must also think of the state of insecurity in African countries that are becoming wastelands for human rights. The fate of millions of refugees, the rise of crass racism, acts of exclusion and expulsion that victimize blacks in societies under-going crises—all these aggravate the condition of African people today. We live in political contexts with a diversity of régimes and ideological options; yet violence and torture appear as methods of exercising power. The African episcopate asks:

> For many of those in the governing groups, has not politics become the very road that leads to dictatorship, totalitarian-ism, and the oppression of the weaker? . . . Freedom of expression and the right to information have become prerog-atives that people enjoy only incompletely or not at all. In countries where constitutions are scoffed at, human beings become the paltry playthings of an uncontrolled power that presses down with all its weight on their souls and bodies.[15]

We are far from the Africa of safaris and official speeches, where the obsession to demonstrate unity and stability serves only to reinforce the power of classes determined to profit as long as possible from their privileges.

This vision of the reality of our people has begun to be recorded in a theological movement developing in black Africa.[16] "Here, we are in Africa, the fatherland of the poor, the weak, and the op-pressed." Cameroonian theologian Engelbert Mveng used these words to open the first colloquium of African and European theologians in Dar es Salaam in 1976. Meeting in Accra in 1977, the Pan-African Conference of Third-World Theologians emphasized "the ill effects of some exploitation of resources by national institu-tions and multinational corporations." While the conference fo-cused little attention on "the roles set aside for women in the churches," it frankly analyzed the overall situation of our people. Many forms of oppression were recognized. "There is the oppres-sion of Africans by white colonialism, but there is also the oppres-sion of blacks by blacks." This analysis led African theologians to clear options: "Theology will deal with the liberation of our people from cultural captivity." The Accra colloquium went even further: "Oppression is found not only in culture, but also in political and economic structures and the dominant mass media. . . . African theology must also be *liberation* theology."[17]

The stakes are high. A clear understanding of the Christian faith must take place in the context of the life-and-death problems of contemporary Africa, which offer a challenge and a fertile stimulus for the church. For the theologian is called to respond not only to questions raised by the cultural patrimony of our people, but also to questions created by conflicts inherent in the mechanisms and structures of oppression at work in society at large. The conflicts that penetrate our culture and history present serious questions as we work to deepen the faith and experience of God in the life of our people. What happened in Accra in 1977 was, in one sense, the reconciliation of Africa with itself. The history of the continent is not merely a history of slavery and domination; it is also a history of struggle and resistance to oppression—as is witnessed by the protest movements that belong to our people's memory throughout generations.[18]

Given the present situation in black Africa, no hesitation is possible: "we must liberate ourselves from all these situations of captivity," says the declaration of the Accra colloquium. Today African churches must position their faith in the context of struggles for justice and liberation. According to the SECAM meeting in Nairobi in 1978, "Liberation of humanity means decolonization, development, social justice, and respect for inalienable human rights and for basic liberties."[19]

Witnessing to the Lord of Life

A time of challenge is beginning for Christians who have discovered Jesus Christ through the theology of the "salvation of souls." It requires us never again to accept living the gospel in a condition of dependence. Our churches will no longer be able to sit at the tables of the rich in order to bring back only crumbs to the "poor blacks." Our task is to shake off the torpor of overfed societies faced with the growing control of imperialism in Africa. Christians who live among peoples subjected to forces of slavery for long centuries have no choice but to clash with societies that exploit and starve peasants, and subjugate plantation laborers and industrial workers. At this time of a deeper evangelization of the African continent, the churches are confronted with what Paul VI called "situations of economic and cultural neocolonialism sometimes as cruel as the old political colonialism."[20]

The presence of Christianity in Africa will no longer be assured by large gifts from overseas. From now on, what will count is the extent of concern the church shows for human beings in search of justice and liberation. There can be no more questions about presenting ourselves to God with a "borrowed humanity." The inhumanity of our people's condition is what now challenges our faith as Africans. We ask if evangelization has produced sufficient fruits of justice.[21] The structures and the organization of African churches are called into question by the new requirements of its mission. Should churches reproduce a Christian heritage that is artificially maintained by paralyzing the forces destined to bring fresh calls to the gospel? Don't we feel a sense of urgency to set up relevant experiments? The problem of mission has been dominated for a long time by the concern to implant the church through structures of authority; hence the priority accorded to the question of an indigenous clergy and episcopate. But now we must recognize that "a church is not truly implanted among a people until it seeks to establish justice and undertake the works of justice."[22]

The world of the poor and outcast reminds Christians that something has gone wrong in our societies. As changes take place in Africa, that world is the frame of reference for faith at the grassroots. A concern for the poor helps us discover that the meaning of religious faith is historically most essential when it is translated, in Jesus Christ, into a dangerous act of speech (Acts 4:20), testimony, or commitment for justice and for the struggle against the mutual exploitation of human beings. In taking on the tasks of faith, African Christians are called to commit themselves to a long tradition of struggle in favor of the poor. As Cardinal Casaroli said in his message to Catholic students in Montreal in 1984, "We need to imbue ourselves deeply with the history and prehistory of Christianity. The battle for justice, and against injustice, for the sake of the poor is a constant."[23]

Set in the context of our time, the parable of poor Lazarus and the rich man reveals the relevance of the Old Testament to the life of Christian communities: "They have Moses and the prophets; let them listen to them" (Luke 16:29). It is impossible to read the Bible while allowing people to remain poor and exploited. In the face of domination, divine revelation emerges as a freeing of humanity from every form of slavery. This basic message comes through when the Bible is read from the viewpoint of the poor of the earth. In the Old Testament, one who practices justice has already come to know God: "He used to examine the cases of poor and needy. . . . Is not that what it means to know me?—it is Yahweh who speaks" (Jer. 22:16). The death and resurrection of Jesus Christ reveal the power of God in those who are weak and rejected by society. The encounter of Christianity with the real Africa can help the churches rediscover the foundation of their faith in the solidarity of God with our history.

Since the incarnation, we can no longer reach for God without recalling Jesus of Nazareth who took the side of the poor, or without condemning injustice. Jesus Christ is not a perverse God whose name serves to reinforce the process of oppression and to legitimize repression and injustice. In the words of Msgr. Kabanga:

> Jesus is accused and condemned because he dares speak the truth. In his death he is united with those whom society rejects. But Jesus risen becomes for us and for the world a force for liberation, the sign of a new world that is coming and has already begun.[24]

We should think through the actual implications of what Johannes Metz calls "the dangerous and subversive memory" of Jesus Christ. We cannot refer to the gospel outside of our current situation, which results from the collective control of the multinational corporations, the fraud of the ruling classes, and generalized corruption. The face of God is revealed through these realities; the true nature of our world is laid bare by the requirements of the kingdom of justice and liberty.

How can the incarnate Word escape being affected by the African "prisons" from which come cries of the tortured? The light of faith shows us the Son of Man in this world of ours, a world defaced by injustice and oppression. He is truly despised (Isa. 53:3) in all situations that humiliate our people. Likewise, he becomes the refugee fleeing throughout the countries of the African continent. Perhaps we need to redefine our relationship with Christ here where our African grasslands and forests nourish the rich countries. If we are to become men and women whose hands sow hope, we must overcome the distance that separates us from the "little people," and learn to live in real solidarity with those who were defeated throughout our history. To live our faith as an extension of the incarnation requires much more than using the words of our languages or the rhythms of our legs. We must go beyond that and join Jesus himself among the poor and the exploited who witness to the challenges of the gospel in their daily life. The experience of faith cannot avoid what the Archbishop of Lubumbashi calls the "descent into hell"—the movement that brings us back to our people where they still live, waiting for the Messiah Savior. It is important to indicate where life is going and to grasp the needs of a society that form the basis for planning for the future.

We are called to accept the logic of the gospel where "the stone rejected by the builders became a keystone" (Matt. 21:42), for those rejected by our societies are the creators of the future. In order to escape criticism, the forces of domination try to impose silence on those who bring a hope for change. If Christians are to join the poor in their struggle for justice, they must overturn the accepted axioms and tap into the resources for the future that lie in the poor. We must make a commitment, then, to those who risk permanent elimination by society, since they are the ones who incarnate hope for needed changes. If local churches wish to be reborn out of the Africa of the powerless, they must walk on these same paths leading to freedom. In Africa, it is no longer possible to read the Bible from the height of the pulpit, without being ready to listen to what is being said about God when the hungry and the outcasts begin to speak. But when the Bible is read by people who have experienced a real "expropriation" of their own being and are deprived of their rights, it will set free a message of life. This message is not always heard in churches that are not really attentive to the vital concerns of the strangled Africa of today. Religious leaders must stop talking about God in order to let the people find the meaning of faith in their daily lives, where they confront the forces of death. That is the only way to liberate all the riches of a denunciation of the gospel.

One thing is sure. Christians cannot think of Jesus Christ as if they were standing at the end of history. The experience of the cross takes shape and form in the lives of our people. No genuine relationship with the gospel can avoid confronting the sin of the world. The incarnation of the faith makes it impossible for us to interpret our faith as enthusiastically as did the Christians of Corinth. We must reaffirm the scandal of the cross so that we do not fall into the Corinthian illusion that lies in wait for us as soon as we begin to think of the church as some "Island of the Blessed." How can we deny the tragedy of the passion of a people whose side has been taken by the crucified Jesus? There is no way we can live the gospel free from the contradictions of a society. As the Suffering Servant struggled against these contradictions, so are we called to fight against a spectrum of forces that prevent the will of God from being done "on earth as it is in heaven." To believe is to witness to the God who delivers us from all evil. Hence Christians must see themselves under an obligation imposed by the cross to carry out a radical critique of our world—such as it is today and such as it becomes. This examination directs us to real commitments that can turn our history back to the course willed by the Lord of Life. There can be no confession of faith without service to the world, without a sense of responsibility for human beings and life, and without increased militancy.

Christians do not live on nostalgia for lost paradises, but from the call to translate the gospel into social changes, so that our enormous riches and unlimited resources are no longer exploited for the benefit of foreigners and local minorities. The cross is a reservoir of critical demands and calls for change. Is it not the most radical and total refutation of our world today? In the midst of systems of accumulation that block all fraternal life and all sharing of the fruits of the earth, the cross teaches us to see Christ not only as the Lord of worship, whose direct and immediate presence is glorified in retreat centers, but also as the Lord of the world in all its dimensions. Fullness of life for the poor and the oppressed is an undertaking inherent in the Christian confession.

Christianity Must Be Credible

To accomplish such a fundamental undertaking, the appeal to convert individuals cannot be separated from the transformation of unjust structures that have been questioned by Old Testament traditions throughout history. Not long ago, the African bishops explained that evangelism and "human promotion" cannot oppose each other.[25] These tasks of faith must be undertaken in situations where the majority of the people live in misery, where the breadth of the dominating factors affects them "deeply and daily." If Christians attempt to live the gospel and root their lives in the reality of our people's situation, Christians cannot struggle against these dominating forces without standing at the side of the poor.

Faithfulness to the Light of Nations requires us to translate Jesus' victory over sin and death into the life of our people. The Resurrection calls for a gospel declaration against the forces that support poverty and injustice. That is why the irruption of the poor and oppressed upsets the traditional structures of local churches. Solidarity with the "little ones" demands different types of presence and action. The word of God can be heard best in village and slum communities as Christians work to build a society where food, jobs, health care, education, and participation in the joy of living are no longer luxuries reserved for an élite. In that context we can better realize that we cannot change the daily reality "without understanding all the forces of oppression and the causes of corruption that undermine the social order. . . . We must develop a critical ability in ourselves and in our communities of faith that will lead people to reflect on the society in which they live. . . . This inventory of the forms of oppression and the causes of corruption is best carried out collectively and from the base upwards."[26]

In small communities, the faith can be practiced in direct contact with the key situations of daily life. This concern is starting to surface in the African churches. Monsignor Bakole wa Ilunga observed that: "To an even greater extent, Christian communities can become places where people are encouraged to take initiatives. Are they sufficiently aware that agricultural production is above all an act of charity in a time of food shortages?"[27] Another bishop in Zaire, Monsignor Kabanga Songasonga, remarked: "The community does not exist solely for prayer and singing, but also to show itself united in all things, to protect itself, and to assure the salvation of each person."[28] Daily life cannot be reduced to what is called the "pious life." We must accept a confrontation between faith and day-to-day matters. Combating injustice springs naturally from the spiritual and religious realm, as the Synod of Bishops recognized in 1974. And the choices that have to be made in this direction cannot fail to provoke tensions with the forces of inertia at work in society. To condemn the corruption of power and its abuses involves risk, and so we must carefully choose our words. Yet how can a church in solidarity with the pariahs of Africa avoid conflicts with existing structures? We should expect to become an object of intimidation and threats, as did Christ himself when he openly confronted the powers of his time.

Conflict is inherent in any gospel practice. Jesus was harassed and suspect right from the beginning of his ministry. The authorities in Jerusalem sent emissaries to investigate his deeds and actions. They set traps to gather evidence against him (Matt. 22:15, 23). Legal specialists slandered him (Mark 3:22, 30). The tension became more and more acute during the course of his ministry. The Gospel of John tells how Jesus spent more and more time in Galilee. The people began to wonder if he would attend the festival in Jerusalem. "He could not stay in Judaea, because the Jews were out to kill him" (John 7:1, 8, 11). This confrontation reaches a climax in Matthew 23 with a collection of Jesus' condemnations in which he called the scribes and Pharisees "a brood of vipers" and "whitewashed sepulchres." This language is not that of the *griots* who praise the powerful people of this world. The language Jesus used angered those who neglected "the weightier matters of the law—justice, mercy, good faith" (Matt. 23:23). By his life as a servant, Jesus raised questions about the rulers who "lord it over them, and their great men (who) make their authority felt" (Matt. 20:25). No institution can escape this radical questioning.

Continuing the prophetic tradition, Jesus mounted an attack on the temple, which was not only the center of worship but also the seat of power and the place of business where taxes were imposed at the expense of the poor and "little ones" (John 2:13-14). Jeremiah had nearly been lynched for having spoken out against the temple (Jer. 26:11-18). Jesus' attack on this heart of Judaism hastened his own death. His disregard for the authorities led him to call Herod "that fox" (Luke 13:32). His association with prostitutes and tax collectors offended the pious believers. He situated his mission in the context of freeing the poor and oppressed (Luke 4:16-21). His radical choice involved a confrontation with situations incompatible with God's will.

God is revealed in Jesus through the gesture of sharing bread, thus creating the hope of a world of fraternity where such acts of solidarity provide the necessities for all people. The praxis of the Good News lies in the realm of signs that announce the presence of the Kingdom (Matt. 11:4-6); it is then translated into acts that free people from all legalisms and required rituals. Viewed in this way, the gospel of Jesus is seen as the written record of a subversive practice that led to conflicts with the contemporary society.[29] When Christians or churches take up this practice, they should not expect to receive total approval. Jesus is not only the savior of souls, but also the hope of the poor, insofar as he reveals to humanity the true name of the God of the exodus (John 17:6).

In situations where poverty and violence condemn the régimes that produce them, it is not an easy matter to stay vigilant, to exercise discernment, or to keep one's distance from the dominating system. We need fixed points of reference today to safeguard the liberty given us by the truth of the gospel. It is the poor who always show us what has gone wrong in society and what needs to be done. As the cross of Jesus expresses the suffering of the poor, we must take on the conflicts and struggles through which the Kingdom is created. Subjected to the harsh ordeal of the world of injustice and poverty in which they are immersed, African Christians must witness to God's truth by taking seriously those questions deemed unworthy of consideration by a religion of "cheap grace." Christians must be integrated into the reality of our time so they can take up the challenge of a tormented history written in violence; they must also recognize the forms of resistance that are the response of the weak to oppression. Who would be willing to take a stand for an African Christianity that looks down on conflict and remains isolated from the struggles that will determine the nature of the future? Julius Nyerere reminded us that if the church wishes to stand for salvation, given the actual conditions of people in Africa, "It has to be consistently and actively on the side of the poor and unprivileged. It has to lead men towards godliness by joining with them in the attack against the injustices and deprivation from which they suffer."[30]

Throughout history, many believers have died to defend the rights of the poor. Today, young people, peasants, and intellectuals have come to know prison and torture because they dared to protest violations of the right to life. Their witness reminds us of the inhumanity of the black people's condition. It reminds us also that we must not only teach the faith, but confess it as well. Perhaps the great challenge of our era is to coordinate militancy and holiness in an experience of faith that lives at the heart of the conflicts of our societies. As Eboussi Boulaga insists:

> Christianity will never recover its credibility, at least in the eyes of some. It will suffer from unadaptation to an Africa on the move until such time as the deepest, most radical questions are no longer handled by preterition and evasion. African Christianity will always be suspect as a mere religion of the herd, a theatricalization of the continuing subordination of Africa to the West in the neocolonial context of a shameful, cowardly dependency in all areas—social, political, economic, and scientific. Hence we must take the measure of the obstacles that an authentic Christianity will have to surmount. It may be that a Christianity to which the African can respond in soul and conscience will be born only from the ashes of so-called middle-class Christianity.[31]

We must accept the down-to-earth questions that Africa is debating, and agree to get our hands dirty in order to live our relationship with God. We must help men and women try to get food, stay in good health, and find their own voice and initiative to resist the forces that are trying to move them from their own land. This basic work must mobilize us today. The Resurrection cannot remain merely an event of the past, but must become contemporary. For generations humiliated by poverty and oppression, the only form of Christianity that can have any meaning strives to redefine itself in its totality "according to the struggles of the people in their resistance against the structures of domination."[32] To escape from the tragedy of meaninglessness, African Christianity is called to become one body with the struggles of the poor who embody for us the memory of Jesus crucified. Under those conditions, Africans will be able to sing a new song to the God who reigns where people are transformed and, in turn, transform the world.

Before your face, a resurrected Africa
Will tremble with happiness and joy,
Will deploy its forces in a broad and noisy motion,
Multiple and varied, powerful, harmonious, gracious,
Like the innumerable movements of the sea,
The movements of the high, deep forest visited by the
    wind.
Africa old and new will dance the dance of jubilation
To the God of Africa
Unique God of the world.[33]

Notes

1. Paul VI, "Popularum Progressio," 32 in *Gospel of Peace & Justice*, edited by Joseph Gremillion (Maryknoll, NY: Orbis, 1976), p. 396.

2. P. Vilain, *Les Chrétiens et le goulag de la faim* (Paris: 1981).

3. See "L'Afrique des bourgeoisies" in *Le Monde Diplomatique*, November 1981.

4. Meinrad Hebga, "Interpellation des mouvements mystiques," in *L'Afrique et ses formes de vie spirituelle, Actes du deuxième Colloque International, Kinshasa 21-27/11/1983*, 17 (Kinshasa: Faculté de Théologie Catholique de Kinshasa), p. 70.

5. "Notre foi en l'homme, image du Dieu: Déclaration du Comité permanent des évêques du Zaïre," 18, in *La Documentation Catholique* 1822 (17 janvier 1982): 125.

6. Ibid., p. 125.

7. See Hebga, "Interpellation des mouvements mystiques," pp. 69-81.

8. "Notre foi en l'homme, image du Dieu," 1, p. 121.

9. *L'Église d'Afrique parle*, Centre Panafricain J.E.C. de Documentation (Nairobi, 1984).

10. From an address by Rev. Albert Nolan, O.P.

11. "Notre foi en l'homme, image de Dieu," 16, p. 124.

12. "Justice et évangelisation en Afrique," 10 in *La Documentation Catholique* 1818 (1981): 1011.

13. "The Demands of National Sovereignty," May 6, 1980 address to the international diplomatic community at the apostolic nunciature in Nairobi, in *Origins* 10 (May 29, 1980): 31.

14. See my book *L'Afrique des villages* (Paris: Karthala, 1982).

15. "Justice et évangelisation en Afrique," 11: 1011.

16. See A. Ngindu, "Courants actuels de la théologie en Afrique," in the

EAAT colloquium *Église noire et théologie en Afrique du Sud*. See also my *African Cry*, translated by Robert Barr (Maryknoll, NY: Orbis, 1986).

17. "Final Communiqué: Pan African Conference of Third World Theologians, Dec. 17-23, 1977, Accra, Ghana" in *African Theology En Route*, edited by Kofi Appiah-Kubi and Sergio Torres (Maryknoll, NY: Orbis, 1979), p. 194.

18. See A. Mbembe, "Pratiques culturelles et créativité populaire en Afrique noire hier et aujourd'hui," lecture at the Institut Catholique de Toulouse, Nov. 29, 1983.

19. "Justice et paix en Afrique," Déclaration du Symposium des Conférences Épiscopales d'Afrique et de Madagascar, in *La Documentation Catholique* 1751 (5 novembre 1978): 928.

20. Paul VI, "Evangelii Nuntiandi," 30, in *Proclaiming Justice & Peace: Documents from John XXIII to John Paul II*, edited by Michael Walsh and Brian Davies (Mystic, CT: Twenty-Third Pubs., 1984 and London: CAFOD, 1984), p. 216.

21. "Justice et évangelisation en Afrique."

22. Draft text for the assembly of the Symposium of Episcopal Conferences of Africa and Madagascar at Yaoundé, 1981.

23. Message to the students in Montreal, *Osservatore Romano*, Eng. text in 24 Sept. 1984 edition.

24. Kabanga Songasonga, *Je suis un homme* (Kinshasa: Éditions St. Paul, 1977).

25. Éla, J.-M., Luneau, R., and Ngendakuriyo, Chr., *Voici le temps des héritiers. Églises d'Afrique et voies nouvelles* (Paris: Karthala, 1981), p. 207.

26. "Justice et évangelisation en Afrique," Section 28, pp. 1015-1016.

27. Bakole wa Ilunga, *Conditions et voies du développement intégral du Zaïre* (Kananga, Zaïre: Éditions de l'Archidiocèse, 1980), pp. 16-17.

28. Kabanga Songasonga, *Tous ensemble* (Lent 1981), pp. 6-7.

29. See the reflections of the J.E.C. of Cameroon, *Jésus, son peuple et les conflits sociaux*, 1982.

30. Julius Nyerere, "The Church's Role in Society," an address originally given to the Maryknoll Sisters in New York, in *A Reader in African Christian Theology*, edited by John Parratt (London: SPCK, 1987), p. 127.

31. F. Eboussi Boulaga, *Christianity Without Fetishes*, translated by Robert Barr (Maryknoll, NY: Orbis, 1984), p. 56.

32. "Final Communiqué of the Pan African Conference of Third World Theologians," p. 193.

33. J. Mbala in *Des prêtres noirs s'interrogent* (Paris: Présence Africaine, 1956).

Chapter 9

The Generations
of Independence

It is inadequate to state these African problems in the almost superficial way I have done up to now. The post-independence problems of Africa are bigger, their roots deeper, their victims younger. In 1981 the Bishops Conference of Cameroon asked the following question of priests: "In your opinion, what most strongly characterizes the church today in Cameroon?" The answers included "fear," "silence," "complicity," and "timidity." Priests also replied: "The church backs away from the forces of oppression, yet who is better placed to cry out against unfairness and injustice?" or "Silence, and complicity with repressive regimes . . ." or "astonishing silence in the face of abuses of power, especially imprisonment and prison regulations."[1] According to all evidence, these unequivocal answers do not take full account of the situation; they say nothing of the actions or positions taken by a particular pastor or group of bishops in favor of justice. But it is revealing that the people questioned Christians and Christian churches about their attitude toward oppression. This generally happens in all African countries where missionary groups carry out charitable work.

What are the priorities and tasks of the church today? What can be expected from the church as it begins to examine itself and tries to define itself in light of the major issues that disturb the new generations in Africa? What challenges must the church take on in order to be seen as something more than folklore by the young

137

people and cadres who are the seeds of the future? And what challenges must the churches take on to reach village peasants who undergo a series of dominations that trap them in a process of increasing degradation and marginalization? Much is at stake in the answers to these questions.

Because the government's apparatus of power stifles any possibility of open debate on serious problems, it is undoubtedly true that the church does create a free space for study and reflection where it is possible to explore routes out of the current impasse. Our encounter with God in faith demands that we take up the concerns, anxieties, struggles, and hopes of the people of the villages and the urban slums that challenge us. Perhaps our first priority should be to stay attentive to the masses of the hopeless who make up the great multitude of the black shantytowns and countrysides that have been abandoned to famine and misery. How do we prepare ourselves to rethink our faith, to reread the gospel, and to arouse in ourselves a new understanding of human problems in Africa? This must happen if we are to promote the changes required by the desperate situations in our countries, where the separation steadily increases between life in the city and life in the village.

The African Church's Search for a Relevant Faith

Our research on the relevance of our faith in the gospel gives a new orientation to the work of the church in Africa. The church must go further than just questioning faith. It must probe the actual practices of the church, if it is going to redefine itself in relation to the struggles and efforts of black people for a better status in contemporary history. How can the church *be* church within the structures of domination in which Africans must seek their identity? In dealing with these issues, it is important to remember that the Christian communities of Africa are part of what Anselme Sanon called the "Third Church"[2]—the churches of the newly independent countries that have irrupted into world history and in which, perhaps, lie the surprises of a future striving to be born.

The most striking characteristic of the church in Africa is the extremely rapid increase in new converts, whose numbers cannot fail to impress older forms of Christianity that have run out of breath. The proportion of young people present at high Mass in urban or rural parishes is one of the most impressive sights in our churches. Yet the Christian character of our local communities is not entirely above suspicion. What is considered a sign of vitality should perhaps be seen as a source of troubling questions. One might conclude that these so-called "young" churches are like "medieval castles that rich Americans have transported stone by stone to the banks of the Potomac."³ Some of us feel secure, perhaps, because of the "comforting notion that everything essential about how to live in Christ has already been said."⁴ Those willing or eager to move into somebody else's house need do no more than copy what comes from elsewhere, according to the standards of law worked out on the banks of the Tiber. If we want to remain locked up in this universe to which Christianity has linked its destiny, we need only disappear under a white man's mask.

In the last century, Hegel thought that true universality could be realized only in the Germany of his own time. Similarly, in the heart of Christianity, many have long thought that the Catholic Church could be fulfilled only in Europe: the churches of outlying societies would be only a kind of appendix or branch—exact copies of the mother churches. The diversity of the control by Western powers in the life of the African churches is precipitating a serious uneasiness that can no longer be hidden.⁵ We find ourselves in what may be called a "religious concubinage," which results from practicing our faith in a way that does not allow our living spirit to speak. "Christians, how unhappy you are. Mass in the morning, diviner at night! Amulet in your pocket, and scapular round your neck!" This song from Zaire reveals the tragedy of most black African Christians. The entry of African communities into the church is an event within a socio-religious context. For many of those baptized, conversion to the gospel is truly an "ambiguous adventure."

We must seriously face up to the questions that African theologians have been asking at Kinshasa, Kumasi, Abidjan, Nairobi, Ouagadougou, or Yaoundé. To extricate ourselves from the "alienated belief" of which Eboussi Boulaga speaks, many men and women feel the need to rethink Christ and to understand him as he is present in our African history and culture. Colonial Christianity is in crisis, as Mongo Beti has shown in his book, *The Poor Christ of Bomba*.[6] Called to confess our faith in the land God has given us, we African Christians cannot live apart from the creative efforts that mark our people's memory today.

Too many people in African churches feel a kind of betrayal or guilt. Their return to certain practices and beliefs, which had been repressed by the violence of mission Christianity, illustrates the failure and lack of meaning of imported lifestyles, doctrines, and institutions. In these societies in disarray from rapid change, the resurgence of former magico-religious practices, and the proliferation of sects in regions where the Christian presence appeared to be established, challenge the official churches. At this time in our history, we need to take up problems of the people—and this opens up a broad field for those concerned with the incarnation of the gospel in Africa.

Problems for the People—Questions Unanswered by Early Evangelization

The church has to reevaluate its practices, attitudes, and teaching on questions that were left unanswered during the first phase of evangelization. The missionary apostolate "cultivated in Africans only that surface which invited cultivation, leaving fallow a no-man's land bristling with clumps of questions, doubts, hopes, and dissatisfactions of every sort."[7] If we were to start all over, we should seriously reevaluate the realm of the African which was "ignored or pillaged by traditional evangelism."[8] This would be particularly true in regions that were "sacramentalized" rather than truly evangelized.

We now understand very well that it is no longer adequate to organize church work around the given structures of Christianity in a clerical context where ritual tasks consume all missionary energies. Today, Catholic churches baptize twice as many faithful in black Africa as in the United States. Veteran generations of missionaries like to hark back to the time when the Spirit blew like a tornado! Baptisms, confessions, and interminable discussions absorbed the life and ministry of priests. In 1958 in Rwanda, one Catholic priest, a White Father, heard 63,500 confessions—an average of over 200 a day for 300 days.

But when the realities of faith—the practices of the church, such as a rigid form of Christian marriage—are transposed from the Latin church into Africa, they meet failure.[9] Today, as we grow more aware of the need to live our faith in the encounter with other cultures, we must go beyond a ministry of institutions and meet Africans within their daily existence. The churches must face up to the challenge posed by converts who still feel the need to consult diviners or marabouts. What form of Christian life is appropriate in villages and slums where the healer still plays a large role in the peoples' lives?

Why shouldn't the church take Jesus at his word as recorded in the gospel, and exercise the power it has been given to lay on hands and heal the sick (Mark 16:18)? It seems urgent to reevaluate this ministry wherever helpless Africans search for peace and security. We need to reread the Bible itself in light of the African's relationship to the invisible world, so that we may grasp the realm of sickness and healing, and show the power of salvation inherent in the gospel. Meinrad Hebga reminds us that Christians are not defenseless when faced with occult forces. They can "make themselves, under the aegis of Jesus Christ, champions in the struggle against the forces of evil, through prayer and exorcism."[10]

Christian ministry among the poor must also intervene in the world of dreams, a major concern of black Africans who translate the language of the beyond by means of the imaginary. In a world where the African is confronted by the forces of the invisible at work in the universe, the church must find an adequate way of proclaiming the primacy of Christ (Col. 1:15-20). Paul set a good example. Instead of condemning the powers and principalities that were very important to new converts from the Greek world, Paul particularly emphasized the central position of Christ as the source of all salvation. In black Africa, the world of the night and the invisible is perhaps the best place for hearing the good news of Jesus' descent into hell (1 Pet. 3:19-20) and then announcing liberation to the African who feels menaced by occult powers.

In one sense, the African society that the church must encounter is based on socio-medical and magico-religious cultural concepts: particularly those of purification, public confession, veneration of ancestors, the coherent language of spirits, and communication between the visible and invisible. During the present crisis in African society, a confrontation must be launched between Christian sacramentalism and the concrete means by which Africans seek reconciliation with invisible powers and protection from occult forces. The search for concrete happiness under the protection of the ancestors *and* in the light of the gospel must be a concern of the church in Africa. Such a search can lead Africans to grasp the essential faith. Christian communities in Africa must have the courage to abandon the comfort of a missionary praxis organized around centers of worship, and instead take up the specific and radical concerns of people. The church must be concerned with the total person; this implies a complete change of lifestyle, but the church must begin with what makes sense in the overall fixed culture. There is no way around it—the unique symbols of the African world challenge the church daily on the relevance of faith.

Time for a Parting of the Ways

No church tradition has yet exhausted the depths of expression in divine revelation. We must search divine revelation for a way to tell about God in Jesus Christ with the words of our own land and culture. We must patiently elicit from the life of gospel communities an African writing of the Word of God that will be meaningful for the African of today. The reading of the gospel is not yet finished, nor is it our sole task to repeat what others have discovered, thought, and organized, like those parrots captured in our virgin forests. We must learn to dispense with the mediation of foreign forms or we will end up living our relationship to the gospel with a borrowed personality.

Today even Western civilization is unsure of itself. It is discovering that it is only an accident. To overcome its own contradictions, it must have the humility to drink from other springs. In light of the irrationalities of the "mimicry" denounced by Albert Tévoèdjré,[11] we must radicalize this self-doubt of the West. The time in which we are now living challenges the pre-established systems that are trying to impose themselves on Christianity in Africa. We alone can create a way for us to believe, to read the Bible, to celebrate the mystery of salvation, and to organize the life of Christian communities. Instead of always referring to what our masters have thought and to the ways they have pointed out, let us start from the experience of our people, from the socio-historical reality in which *we* are engaged. Instead of taking up ready-made formulas and dogmatized institutions, we prefer to take the risk of being ourselves and the adventure of speaking out from the exact context where we are seeking new paths.

What is heard in the local churches of Africa still sounds too much like an echo of an old world and looks too much like a reflection of foreign life. A Christianity that does no more than imitate is powerless to resolve our problems, because it is cut off from our own realities. If Christianity just repeats previously articulated doctrines that have been objectivized and institutionalized, it will only contribute to the development of pure passive receptivity in Africans, who will become incapable of examining or creating anything for themselves. The Risen One exposes faith to an inexhaustible realm of possibilities. That is why we are searching for a form of speech that will bring the voices of Africa to the life of the world-wide church. Hence, we should not say anything, think anything, or do anything in the church unless it springs from daily reality, from the living traditions of the African peoples, or from the concrete tasks of villages and slums.

Today the expression and encountering of differences should mobilize the African church to take on the historical task of reshaping the universal church, using our knowledge and the documents and tools of our setting. This is an enormous task for the men and women of Africa who are compelled to undertake new beginnings, and who are called to live their faith as a moment of ongoing creation. It is incumbent on us to experience the meaning of Christianity, and to liberate its catholicity as it unfolds in the incessant genesis of humanity and of a world stirred up by the dynamism of the Spirit. A time is dawning for the Christian communities of Africa in which they can rediscover their living memory, their initiative, and their imagination in order to "reinvent the church." This will be done as these communities confront themselves, moving from the past and the present into the unknown future that challenges us.

Where Do We Begin?

All of this presupposes a body of research and experience here in Africa, as well as a reconsideration of the methods of oral style and a reactivation of African "palaver" in announcing the gospel through religious instruction and evangelization. The translation of the Word of God into African languages and cultures becomes a game of exchange and reciprocity between the Christian message and unwritten cultural traditions. An entire reservoir of words, images, symbols, and concrete categories can cause a new Christian vocabulary to burst forth from the encounter between the church and African society. The catechetical and liturgical vocabulary coming from Africa can result in the birth of a theological language rooted in the cultures of our soil.

The total sacramental nature of the Christian mystery and its basic symbolism need also to be rediscovered from our own cultural rooting.[12] But until we close the epoch of the minute prescriptions of canon law, no celebration of the liturgy and sacraments can be enriched by using elements of the African setting. In black Africa, for example, baptismal initiation and the rite of marriage must confront the customs of initiation and the matrimonial traditions of each human group. We cannot think of the basic elements of Christian worship as manufactured goods exported throughout the world according to invariable and uniform standards. A church in search of maturity cannot be satisfied with consuming cultural and liturgical traditions that belong to a prescribed church model. If the church is to speak the language of communion, it must stop its discourse of uniformity so that the pentecost of nations may emerge.

This leads to a troubling question put into words by Anselme Titianma Sanon of Bobo-Diolaso, Burkina Faso: "Does not the implantation of worship in a culture include the use of the fruits of the earth and human labor? How far is the use by Jesus of the fruits of wheat and the vine normative until the end of time?"[13] These questions do not come from hotheads, but from pastors of souls who see in the church "the most favorable environment for expressing and translating the richness of the encounter between Christian universalism and the particularity of different cultures."[14]

People and their languages differ. It seems that this recognition of diversity is fundamental today. What is the Spirit saying to the churches of Africa? Shouldn't we listen even more carefully for the voice of the Spirit, so as to speak the same faith under different forms and signs? If God meets all human beings in the singularity of their condition and culture, shouldn't we also follow Paul's advice to "stay as they were before God, at the time of their call" (1 Cor. 7:24)? These questions converge on "African Christianity," which Paul VI designated as the work of the African churches during his trip to Kampala in 1969. John Paul II, in turn, told the bishops of Zaire, "Africanization is *your* task." This project "covers wide and deep fields which have not yet been sufficiently explored, whether it is a question of the language to present the Christian message in a way that will reach the spirit and heart of Zaireans, of catechesis, theological reflection, the most suitable expression in liturgy or sacred art, or community forms of Christian life."[15] This vast enterprise must make "Christ himself an African through the members of his body," in the words of the pope in Kenya. We should rejoice in the interest Rome has shown in our quest to mobilize the living forces of the African church. In August 1985, John Paul II reminded us in Cameroon that "a break between the gospel and culture would be dramatic."[16]

The Pitfalls of Africanization

Yet there are pitfalls in Africanization that we should be aware of, and that have caused quite a stir in the churches. In the words of I. De Souza, "This topic concerns African Christians, pastors, and theologians. They need to be directed so they do not take up matters that could disturb the order and balance of social life in the new states of Africa." As if we had nothing else to do but to rediscover our languages and rhythms, our art and symbols! As if Christian communities had no concerns but to take up whatever is attractive or good, just or valuable in our ceremonies, customs, and institutions! The generations of *négritude* will not be easily satisfied with a limited statement of faith, which reduces the realm of investigation to "a certain approach to the Christian mystery on the basis of Africans' reactions and ways of thinking."[17]

In fact, an enormous body of reflection and research along these lines is going on in seminaries, pastoral and catechetical centers, institutes of higher education for religious culture, and faculties of theology. The research focuses on the confrontation between the gospel and the vast realm of African authenticity. Efforts at renewal in the ministry of the church that have revived African communitarianism fulfill this major objective. An individualistic presentation of the questions of salvation leaves the African helpless. Christian ceremonies seem to have been unable to create true links of solidarity that extend into the invisible world and promise peace to people faced with the adversities of life. Hence, there is a need to re-create small communities, within which Christians can find security about all dimensions of their being through collective decision-making. Priority has been given everywhere to village and shanty-town communities. Because they seem to be the great hope of churches with too few ordained ministers, the task of awakening and training these communities tends to become the major concern of the African church. In former times, the missions themselves were often nothing more than a filling-station for religious needs; today, however, the church is obliged to shift the focus of its life and action toward small communities where the faith can be lived concretely through well-defined commitments.

If the Christians of a particular place direct the whole life of the church as they live their faith and the gospel, they will be able to give up the individualistic features of a civilization of the "anti-brother," which leads to an impersonal religious life. Lived in a Western style, the Christian mystery can disorient Africans in their relationship with God, with their brothers and sisters and with the universe. Yet whenever the Christian faith incorporates and lives the African values of communion and solidarity, with their specific requirements and implications, this enlarged community has a positive impact on the health of human relationships. In fact, it is precisely this option for community that governs all the contemporary questions about evangelization in Africa today.

The bishops of Africa and Madagascar have declared:

> The building up of our churches must be carried out with constant reference to the life of communities. These communities will help us bring to the universal church not only our particular cultural and artistic experiences . . . but also our own theological thought, which will try to resolve the questions posed by our different historical contexts and by the way our societies have evolved.

But faith lived in an African setting is a dangerous mystification if the church is closed in on itself, and confronts only the problems of its cultural identity. The language of Africanization has become terribly ambiguous. It can also offer security to those authorities who fear that, through their solidarity and commitment to the poor and oppressed, African Christians might proceed to question the totality of neo-colonial exploitation present in the newly independent countries. If the churches of the continent focus only on seeking an authentically African Christianity, the process of stripping Africa of its riches will continue unabated. As Aimé Césaire once said ironically about a famous book: "You're going to the Congo? Pay your respects to Bantu philosophy!" After independence, the theory of *négritude* was rescued in certain countries to legitimate a policy of making use of technical assistance. "You have the sense of the sacred," we were told, "and you will help save the world from materialism." While Africans were enclosed in this language of *négritude* and shut off from real life, others moved into the more important realms of economics and politics.

Similarly, a liturgy using indigenous music might cause Africans to forget that they are human beings under domination. Expressing their calvary through the rhythm of their own music may give them the hope of celestial happiness—as happened through Negro spirituals in America. When Christianity was implanted in Africa, something important happened at the same time: while the converts were distracted by the Bible thrust into their hands, their land was stripped from them. Even the salvation announced by missionaries was envisaged only in the context of a religion of the beyond. In the words of the poet Paul Niger, "Jesus stretched out his hands over these curly heads, and the Negroes were saved. But certainly not here on earth!"

The rhythm of drums and *balaphons* within our churches cannot shelter us Africans from the threats of the "weapons of food" brought to bear on peasants crushed by the dictatorship of peanuts, cocoa, and cotton. The famine of the Sahel appears to be not so much a natural calamity or an outcome of climate as a result of a policy of oppression and domination over peasants and herdsmen.[18] In these countries, the church must make it a priority to be African in its "being" as well as in its "appearance." We must not expend all our strength wondering if we need to think like Descartes to be a theologian. Instead, we must feel the need to leave libraries and offices, and move toward a type of society where the intellectual works among the planters, the university student among illiterates, the physician among bush people, and the theologian or pastor among villagers—there where hunger, misery and despair become a future leading nowhere but to the road of revolution. Most often the Africans who seek to adapt Christianity are those who have become strangers to their villages, in the same way that uprooted intellectuals seek "*négritude*." Like them, to paraphrase Fanon, African theologians or pastors who decide to seek "the road of indignity will bring back from their adventures only terribly fruitless formulas. They will attribute privilege only to customs, traditions, modes of appearance; and their labored and painful quest will yield nothing in the end but a banal striving for the exotic."[19]

Taking on the Challenges of Tomorrow's Generations

Too many obstacles prevent African Christians from setting themselves up as a showcase or from seeing themselves as others see them. If it is true that we should not seek our future in the past of others, we must not forget that culture is not something fixed once and for all for a given group of people. Rather, culture is the expression of the life of a people at a given time in history, with continuities and breaks, tensions, and challenges. If we are to join Africans in their daily existence, we must first restore African culture's real dimension, its tragedies and its struggles, and the internal discords and contradictions on which it is built. Since black priests first began to question Christianity, they have too frequently used a type of "anti-colonialist" jargon. Today we must be wary of this type of talk. When nourished by the work of Western ethnologists, it tends to become an official ideology, justifying and reinforcing the current domination by the states. The intellectuals who generate this ideology are often nothing more than the *griots* of the ruling power.

How can we believe in Jesus Christ when the affluent nations refuse to recognize that our black peoples have a position within history? Jesus of Nazareth asks us: "Africans, who do you say I am?" and we must answer from our world of today. The answer must come from our tragic situation that we must recognize. In a few trenchant phrases, the Swiss sociologist Jean Ziegler summarized the varied schemes focused on Africa today:

What is happening is this. Africa has been promoted to the dignity of becoming the privileged parade-ground for the struggles of global forces and the new battlefield for multinational interests. A gigantic political-economic safari allows it to be used to satisfy every greed. As the last zone of the planisphere with an open hunting season, it is prey for the organized hunts of some and the poaching of others.[20]

How can we express our belonging to God in a continent that does not belong to itself? Under the pretext of cooperation, economic and financial organizations freely quarrel over our lands and beaches, our bauxite, copper and diamond mines, and our business and tourism—without neglecting our uranium, oil, and of course, the very conscience of our people. Given this situation today, must we let ourselves be locked up in a religious universe whose three dimensions are sin, the sacraments, and grace?

What is our purpose then in mobilizing base communities? The phenomenon of recolonization in Africa is developing a new proletariat in the cities and the countryside. The capital cities grow like an enormous cancer, and are becoming a formidable powder keg ready to explode. Waiting for another world should not divert us from what is going on in Africa today, where, as John Paul II said to the diplomatic corps at Kinshasa in 1980, "This continent, too, is marked by influences directed from inside and outside, often under cover of economic aid, but actually in the perspective of an interest that has nothing really humanitarian about it but its label."[21]

The Kingdom of God will take root and establish itself only within history. How can we express this Kingdom concretely under current conditions in our countries where the real but secret empire of financial power and capital has reduced a fabulously rich continent to a pauper? It is true, of course, that a kind of "bush" Christianity has been planted in Africa, in spite of urban growth. Priests can be seen travelling from village to village to distribute the sacraments—usually to the largest number of Christians possible. In these villages, the life of the church is basically oriented toward worship, devotions, morality, catechetical instruction, and the sacraments. But even so, ecclesiastics are rarely found among the peasants, helping with problems arising from their work on the plantations.

Today the governing classes, assisted by agricultural technicians, are organizing peasant societies with an eye to the interests of the former colonizers and the interests of the bureaucracy in the capital cities. The prosperity of the cities and the growing middle classes owes much to the sweat of the peasants. Any presence of the church in Africa must take this into account. The countryside supports the burden of growth while receiving few of its benefits. Julius Nyerere, then president of Tanzania, expressed his concern that "if we are not careful, we can arrive at a situation where . . . the true exploitation . . . will be that of the peasants by the city-dwellers."

How is the church to find a niche in rural areas at a time when the disparagement of peasant systems of agriculture has reached the point of planned chaos? This has happened in Chad and northern Cameroon where planners encourage the growth of cotton instead of millet, and in Ivory Coast where the most modern methods of growing rice produce hunger.[22] These modern planners who want to regulate the market in foodstuffs have succeeded no better than the old illiterate traders. The church must reexamine its attitudes and actions so they will truly benefit defenseless populations who are caught up in so-called rural modernization that usually serves only to bring peasants into the machinery of capitalism, which, in turn, places them squarely on the road leading to the catastrophe of hunger. The church must deal with questions of African villages—questions which cannot be limited to matters of beliefs and traditional ceremonies thought to be incompatible with the Christian faith. How can we announce the message of the Beatitudes to peasants backed into a corner? At a time when everything is centralized in the capital cities, and when decisions about state structures are rarely based on the needs of the peasant masses (the bulk of our population), the church cannot be content to enlarge prayer groups and develop forms of devotions and piety inherited from nineteenth century Europe. Today we must try to build a bridge between the memory of our people and the challenge of tomorrow, a bridge that can be crossed by the new generations.

Africa is changing. Cities are growing; rural development is generally conceived of today as the growing of export crops; and the rural world is reduced to a sector that produces revenue to pay for the consumption of urban minorities. But all these changes provide a privileged terrain for evangelization. In societies where the imposition of agro-industrial conglomerates carries the seed for private appropriation of the land, landless peasants are forced to migrate to the cities, worsening inequities, and proliferating shanty-towns on the edges of large cities. This failure resulting from the socio-economic decisions of newly-independent African states also constitutes an appropriate setting for the mission of the church in Africa.

We can no longer read the gospel in any place other than among the peasant masses who are today the most miserable, the most exploited and undernourished class. They bear the burden of growth, producing export crops that allow the collection of taxes and the accumulation of foreign exchange—both of which accrue in the end to the state, that is, the governing bureaucracy. We cannot ask questions about the meaning and the demands of faith while behaving as if no gulf exists between the standard of living of the affluent urban minority and that of the disinherited majority—the pariahs of African independence. We must experience our faith in this crisis of Christianity, both in the bush and in the challenge of the expanding African cities. We are the victims of circumstances, yet all these questions must be addressed by the church in Africa as part of the process by which it is renewed and rejuvenated.

Can Christianity Be Based on the "Periphery"?

In black Africa, there's no doubt that the church has always served the defenseless populations through educational, social and health-related projects. But it is also true that where secondary schools and hospitals were originally founded to help the poor, they have usually ended up within the reach only of families belonging to the upper classes. In many parts of Africa, Christian missions do participate in numerous activities to organize and popularize Christianity in the countryside. But as the church meets concrete needs, perhaps it should also avoid being cut off from the concrete realities, which would be something incompatible with the Christian faith. Surely the training of people should be the primary task in our countries. In the end, the church should promote developmental practices at the grassroots level, and support the struggles of the poor to change society. If the church sees itself as being above socio-political and economic conflicts, it will remain in the imperialist camp, and help integrate Africa into a system of domination whose victims are the peoples of the "periphery."

The church's socio-economic and charitable activities indicate that it seems to have adopted a policy of "underdevelopment," which in many ways constitutes a spreading hoax, to the extent that it likens underdevelopment to a slowing-down. In fact, this vision of the church places it outside the real movement of history and the dialectic of internal and external social contradictions. In the end, it comes down to no more than a policy of assistance and "modernization"—which really means some expansion of the capitalist sector at the expense of more distortion, disequilibrium, dependence, and a further marginalization and impoverishment of the masses. Everywhere in Africa a chasm yawns between the capital cities and the back country, the élite and the masses, the state and the people!

The African neo-colonial state of today, ravaged by corruption, has taken over the use of violence, formerly a weapon of the colonialists. Now, as then, the insolent machinery of the state operates with a force that is senseless, blind, and savage. Unchallenged, it reigns over hearts and minds, in an atmosphere where distrust and fear have become an actual dimension of the collective consciousness. The African church is in the presence of human beings whose hands are empty—men, women, and young people with no future, permanently kept in the dark by newspapers that are monopolized by authorities searching for popular legitimacy.

Given these conditions, if we do not want the Christian message to be used to anesthetize the consciousness of the poor and humble, we had better find ways to manifest the subversive power of the gospel.[23] Because the church has compromised itself in the past by dealing with financial powers and by setting up systems of unfair exchange, the incarnation of Christianity in Africa today should be seriously questioned from the point of view of the poor and oppressed. The church has meaning *only* if it becomes the place where the cry of the people is heard, in the same way that Jesus Christ reactualized the acts of the God of the exodus.[24] In Africa, where the rich oppress the poor and then further enrich themselves at the expense of the poor, the many forms of corruption are a cancer eating away at the ruling classes. We must urgently and forcefully repeat again and again that "to oppress the poor is to insult their

Creator" (Prov. 14:31). All around us, groups of the majority live in unjust situations that "cry out for God's attention," in the words of Paul VI in *Populorum Progressio*. How shall we conquer the hunger and inequities that obsess Africans today and that result from a strategy of domination?[25] By charitable works? What "gospel" reactions are called for by the dependence in which most Africans live? Do we offer aid or liberation? Instead of monopolizing initiatives through projects designed elsewhere, we should free the creativity of villages and communities by launching credible alternatives and genuine "substitute authorities."

The church is called to be vigilant. It is invited to show courage. It must abandon the beaten paths of a praxis that shuts it up in a kind of "dogmatic slumber." When this happens, the church remains unaware of human rights violations, blind harassment, mutilations, and structures of inequality and domination among peoples. The church no longer sees how the neocolonial system extends its long tentacles with the complicity of national bureaucracies, while the insolent and scandalous prosperity of a tiny segment of the élite leads to homelessness for an increasing number of young people and adults. If the church wants to be present in the current history of Africa, it had better understand that its identity is at stake among all levels of African society, including thousands of African youths who cannot turn their backs on their families of peasants and workers without being immediately coopted by the club of the "haves" who live off the exploitation of the disinherited social classes. The church must be of one body with all those deprived of their rights or reduced to silence—if it is indeed the body of the Crucified One of Golgotha.

In our environment, our faith does not ask questions about the sex of the angels or the infallibility of the pope; instead we question the lack of any genuine application of the critical function inherent in the Christian faith. How can we show that the African church is blocked by an ecclesiastical praxis that is, in fact, a kind of museum of a narrow moralism, a ritualistic sacramentalism, a disembodied spirituality, and a withering dogmatics? If God is revealed through history, those who are absent from the history of our time are also the recipients of the revelation of the living God. How can God intervene in our world when young people throw the few resources they have into education, and end up learning in a system that ensures the continuation of social classes and social inequities? The increasing marginalization of vast groups of people is where the church should manifest and define its creativity and its mission in Africa.

If we do not want to set countless human beings adrift in the many sects that manipulate the gullible, or throw them into the hands of "spiritual masters" and traffickers in occult powers who disseminate alienating ideologies, we must liberate African Christianity from its Babylonian captivity. Christianity in Africa has been made captive by Roman structures that are weighed down by an ecclesiastical mentality; by the sociological burden of a religion of the "other world"; by forms of piety and devotion of Christianity in decay; by the disguised apolitical stance of Western missionaries; by the massive apathy, irresponsibility, and intolerable greed of certain members of the clergy; by the disembodied spirituality of some indigenous lay people; and by the lack of awareness or infantilism of African religious trained in a European fashion. Ever since the slave trade, the history of Africa has been a history of violence, characterized by harassment and by contempt for humanity. In Africa the church cannot hover over the conflict, looking down, and aspiring to a transcendence of the Spirit. It must regain contact with the African soil; not only with African religions and cultures, but with the humiliations, with the violence of imperialism and political authorities, and with the resistance and struggles of the people.

Situations of injustice and domination in Africa demand that the church take notice of the social functions of faith and theology that are being shaped by the risks and uncertainties of daily struggles in solidarity with the oppressed and outcast of African society. This form of faith and theology *is* relevant. It demands that we question pastoral projects that consider only such problems as priestly and religious vocations, polygamy, marriage ceremonies, and the like. We in the church simply must realize that all strategies of aid totally ignore the radical issue of the mechanisms that engender and perpetuate poverty and misery. There is a risk today that creating and engaging in works of charity may placate the church's conscience by closing its eyes and ears to alienating social conflicts. The church has done little to equip itself with tools to analyze the present situation so that it can study what it is doing in light of the gospel. Similarly, the church has done little to create an authentic ministry of Christian understanding focused on the current problems of our society.

Above all we feel the need to decipher the meaning of our contemporary history in relation to the efforts of our people to build a new future for themselves, a future different from the colonial past and from the neo-colonial present. We need to study that history, confronting it with the practice of Jesus described in the gospel as a living and real narrative. From now on, our starting point for meeting reality should not be eternal truths, but rather forms of commitment that actualize the way in which Jesus existed among the people of his time. The transformation of African society is the context for this confrontation between the African reality and the requirements of the gospel. We must put ourselves back at the center of life where the future is bursting forth, and share in its creation.

Only the commitment of the church to dispossessed peasants, unemployed young people, the populations of shanty-towns, and the forces within society that have been neutralized or reduced to silence until now—only this kind of commitment can demonstrate that the gospel is truly liberating and heralds a new future. As part of this commitment, the African people must likewise be reborn as a group. As Paul VI wrote:

> The Church has the duty to proclaim the liberation of millions of human beings, many of whom are her own children—the duty of assisting the birth of this liberation, of giving witness to it, of ensuring that it is complete.[26]

The "little ones" are discovering that the era of African independence has brought nothing but unemployment, a loss of buying power, insecurity caused by uncontrolled elements of government, daily difficulties, and a growing gap between their standard of living and that of the governing classes. As this happens, what should we do? Which side should the church take in African countries where nothing basic has changed, and where the sole contribution of independence has been to replace classical colonial structures with oppressive structures that are more complete and less direct? Don't our baptism and confirmation force us to take a stand against anything that can block Africa's future or that can threaten the rights of its people or the dignity of their existence? Today Africans have given themselves new masters with black skin. And meanwhile peasants discover that independence works only for the barons of corrupt régimes, businessmen, experts, merchants, and administrative or political authorities. How are we to perceive, critically, what is at stake in the incarnation in Africa today?

Our adherence to Christ undergoes a harsh testing in this situation where bloody dictatorships spring up in the shadow of international cooperation, and where instances of successful decolonization become only another fair target for imperialism. These systems can be considered the primary cause of misery and oppression in the African countries. The church will need to perform acrobatic feats to escape the crucial questions posed by this situation. Isn't helping with the birth of the liberation of humanity in Africa the most immediate and the most urgent historical task of the church? Wouldn't it be the truly prophetic response and a sign of hope for people living in despair?

The African church needs to find a way to live the gospel in the midst of violence and misery, knowing that God identifies with the miserable. Today Jesus is each oppressed person. We must rediscover the rooting of Christ in the living conditions of Africans; and, through the crucifixion, rediscover the tragedy of the black people, where every hut is its own calvary. Faith has no meaning until we can reflect the glory of the One who has "called you out of darkness into his own wonderful light" (1 Peter 2:9).

The Role of African Christian Youth

The church must be able to count on Christian youth to witness to this gospel in a world seeking justice and liberty. They must be able to reject opportunism and an emphasis on careers. They cannot be like the former militants of student organizations, who, for the most part, abandoned their ideals of struggle and their search for a freer and more caring society by wearing themselves out in a frantic accumulation of luxuries, using all kinds of tricks to mask their internal contradictions. During this period of change in African society, thousands of young people in large cities have thrown themselves on an opiate that cures boredom and comforts unemployment by its "qualitative" leap into the artificial paradises created by the gods of Europe and America. The cinema, based on escape and materialism, has become a key feature of the mass subculture and an actual school for crime for budding juvenile delinquents in crowded urban settlements. It is also a significant obstacle to the awakening of consciences about the serious problems that face newly independent African countries. We must deal with the questions of African youth; they will become the ruling cadres, businessmen, thinkers, and artists who will determine Africa's destiny.

In black Africa, youth is a variable force; it can be a decisive contribution in resisting external and internal factors of domination. Because our neocolonial structures have removed any real content from the idea of independence, it would be a great tragedy if Africa's young people, students, and intellectuals were to separate themselves from the mass of the people. What will happen if they shut themselves up in the artificial environment of air-conditioned offices without ever being involved in the land of the pariahs—the peasants and the masses who crowd together in the huts of urban complexes? African youth is generally a non-privileged social group that also suffers from the contradictions of blocked societies (as witnessed by numerous strikes in most African countries). But the task of Africa's Christian youth, students, and intellectuals must be to join the peasant and worker masses, to learn from them, and to participate in their struggle. If this happens, the coming victory of a second independence will no longer benefit just an élite.

The option for the poor and oppressed by African Christian youth must be seen as the response of the gospel to the immense clamor of a continent. We have to incarnate that response in the places of tension and conflict in our societies, reminding ourselves that the future belongs to those who can give the present generations reasons to live and to hope. Then, in the new mornings of a new world, Africa will sing out its newly-won dignity and its rediscovered freedom.

Notes

1. Conférence Épiscopale Nationale du Cameroun (CENC), *Dossier sur la vie spirituelle des prêtres*, July 1981, p. 103.

2. See Anselme Titianma Sanon, *Tièrce église, ma mère* (Paris: Beauchesne, 1972).

3. F. Eboussi Boulaga, *"Métamorphoses africaines," Christus* 77 (January 1973).

4. Meinrad Hebga, *Émancipation d'églises sous tutelle* (Paris: Présence Africaine, 1976), p. 159.

5. See an analysis in *Civilisation noire et Église catholique* (Paris: Présence Africaine, 1978).

6. Mongo Beti, *The Poor Christ of Bomba* (London: Heinemann, 1971).

7. Sidbe Semporé, "Les Églises d'Afrique entre leur passé et avenir," *Concilium* 126 (1977), p. 23. Translated by Sarah Fawcett as "The Church in Africa between Past and Future" in *Concilium* 106 (1977), pp. 1-25.

8. Ibid.

9. See M. Legrain, *Mariage chrétien, modèle unique? Questions venues d'Afrique* (Paris: Chalet, 1978).

10. See Meinrad Hebga, *Sorcellerie et prière de délivrance* (Abidjan & Paris: INADES and Présence Africaine, 1982).

11. "Upside Down or The Folly of Mimicry" in *Poverty: Wealth of Mankind* by Albert Tévoèdjré (Oxford: Pergamon, 1979), pp. 26-51.

12. See Chapter 3 above for this whole question.

13. Anselme Titianma Sanon, "Message universel dans la pluralité culturelle," *Concilium* 135 (1980), p. 110. Translated by Francis McDonagh as "The Universal Message in Cultural Plurality," *Concilium* 135 (1980), p. 91.

14. Ibid., p. 94.

15. John Paul II, speaking to the Bishops of Zaire, "Bring the Authentic Gospel to the African Cultures" in *Modern Missionary Documents and Africa*, edited by Raymond Hickey (Dublin: Dominican Publications, 1982), p. 257.

16. John Paul II, "The Cry of Authentic Liberation," *Origins* 15 (August 29, 1985): 171.

17. I. De Souza, in *Peuple du Monde* 91 (1976): 41-43.

18. See the works cited in Chapter 5, note 7 above.

19. Frantz Fanon, *The Wretched of the Earth*, translated by Constance Farrington (New York: Grove Press, 1966).

20. Jean Ziegler, *Main basse sur l'Afrique* (Paris: Seuil, 1978).

21. John Paul II in *L'Osservatore Romano* (English edition), May 19, 1980, p. 4.

22. For a discussion of these problems, see René Dumont and Marie-France Mottin, *L'Afrique étranglée* (Paris: Seuil, 1980), pp. 217-221. Translated from the French by Viviene Menkes as *Stranglehold on Africa* (London: A. Deutsch, 1983).

23. Vincent Cosmao, *Changing the World: An Agenda for the Churches*, translated by John Drury (Maryknoll, NY: Orbis, 1984), pp. 59-62.

24. See my *African Cry*, translated by Robert Barr (Maryknoll, NY: Orbis, 1986).

25. See the survey in *Jeune Afrique*, May 12, 1980.

26. Paul VI, "Evangelii Nuntiandi," 30 in *Proclaiming Justice & Peace: Documents from John XXIII to John Paul II* (Mystic, CT & London: Twenty-Third Publications and CAFOD, 1984), p. 216.

Chapter 10

Speaking about God to Africans

It is not easy to grasp the full range of problems concerning faith that are emerging from the African churches. For some years now, the media seem to have blotted out whatever is being said about God in the heart of our villages, on the grounds that it is not supported by Scripture or by pressure groups within the church. Similarly absent are the commentaries and reflections that well up from assemblies and meetings where peasant men and women, small-scale artisans, manual laborers, or intellectuals gather together around the gospel. At best, certain themes are noticed and included in discussions at institutions; beyond these themes, other talk seems foreign, as if it were inappropriate to our identity. In short, whatever comes out of Africa does not carry much weight in contemporary discussions about God.

Yet a zest for life and freedom deeply marks black awareness. In the face of all the ordeals, humiliations and sufferings that form our memory, we cannot help repeating the question that God asked Cain: "Where is your brother Abel? What have you done? Listen to the sound of your brother's blood, crying out to me from the ground" (Gen. 4:9-10). In this situation of death, certainly familiar to us as Africans, the question of Christ crucified becomes part of us. Today many of our people feel that even God has rejected them: "My God, my God, why have you forsaken me?" Will the blessing promised to all the nations of the earth stop before it reaches us?

160

Will God be absent from the experience of black people in human history? Will discussions in today's church include this absence? My concern now is to invite churches and Christians to bring God back into our midst and locate God at the heart of a new covenant in which we will be concretely involved. Talking about God begins when God becomes present again among us. All of this needs clarification so that we can learn again how to talk about God to our fellow Africans.

What could be the "proper identity of an African theology"? Presented with a question like this, I feel a certain uneasiness. We must be careful not to engage in only an academic exercise, a ritual, and bypass the fundamental questions that besiege us. In one sense, African theology is still at a stage where it must question itself. Should it opt for adaptation or incarnation? This dilemma faces the church today, as do other serious questions. We cannot generate an African theology for a small minority of the privileged or indulge in the luxury of reflecting about the gospel for its own sake, without ever thinking about the people to whom it is addressed. Instead we must invest our resources in theological work that seeks out people right where they are in their own universe, and helps them reflect on the relation between the gospel and their specific life, with all of its complexity, its dimensions, and its requirements.

It would be unhealthy to become complacent with our rhetoric about dead issues, stifled hopes, about the dangers of the debasement of our societies, or the neglect of people who demand emancipation and liberty. Our debate on "African theology" cannot be reduced to a command performance for external consumption, which responds to distant concerns or to a range of problems quite foreign to the fate of those who are often left out of our discussions—the peasant men and women of black Africa. We must resist the Byzantine "palaver" of academic discussions on chimerical subjects. African theology can be affirmed only by renouncing intellectual prostitution or religious talk for financial gain. The urgent needs of Africa reject every excuse we can manufacture.

I should like to outline a process and identify some clusters of tension. It is from this point that Africa is summoned to speak about that God whose final word is Jesus Christ, the ultimate revealer. We need to reappropriate creatively the meaning of this basic event, but we cannot isolate the incarnation from the body of questions that impose a set of problems, themes, ways of research, and a special language. The goal of these reflections is to locate precisely where we must be in order to organize discussion about faith on the basis of our situation as Africans.

Requirements of Our Faith as Africans

The debate on African theology arose some years before Vatican II.[1] By now one fact has been established: we no longer need to discuss the principle of the possibility or legitimacy of an African theology. The principle has been established. Appeals have come from the magisterium itself, inviting Africans to assume their own responsibilities for building a theology incarnated in the living thought of the men and women of our continent. Vatican II stated that theological investigation must be undertaken in each great socio-cultural region.[2] If theologians are to exercise their specific ministry in the service of Christian communities, they must free themselves from all dogmatism, and open themselves to the life of a people and to the questions and requests of an age, in order to interpret Jesus' message in the context of the people to whom that message is addressed. Thus, according to the Council, the entirety of revelation must undergo a new examination.

At the time of his first trip to Africa, John Paul II recognized that theological reflection was one of the areas of Africanization that had not been sufficiently explored. As was emphasized by the African bishops after the Synod of 1974, theological reflection is a fundamental requirement of the faith from which the churches of Africa cannot hide. The bishops insisted on the importance of an African theology open to the fundamental aspirations of the peoples of the black continent.[3] The internal situation of the African churches obliges us to undertake theological work that responds to these aspirations.

Is it necessary once again to describe the tragedy of churches born from Western expansion to conquer the world by establishing alliances of political strength and cultural power?[4] Speaking to the bishops of Zaire, John Paul II emphasized the importance of the content of faith, how best to express it, and how to relate theology and faith. For a long time, missions have been concerned with transferring Christian ideals into the "new worlds," dreaming of restoring the unity of faith, culture, and lifestyle that was already disintegrating in the heart of old Europe. We have inherited a church whose mental structures were shaped by a decadent scholasticism. How can we ignore the theological vacuum in which African churches set out on their arduous journey? Until recently, most priests in training in mission countries had only Tanqueray's manuals to stimulate their theological reflection. It is difficult to imagine the shocking situation of theological underdevelopment that gave birth to local Christian communities. Nor did the anti-intellectualism of numerous missionary groups stimulate a spirit of inquiry! Wherever the overriding concern of the ecclesiastical authorities has been to plug up the holes in parishes without priests, many of the faithful are stranded after completion of catechetical instruction for first communion. The result, in the courageous words of Sidbe Semporé, is that "We lack theologians and, in consequence, an appropriate theology."[5]

Although the missionary impulse came from the churches of the "Center," Christian communities should now be given true autonomy at the same pace as their people. They should not be condemned to a condition of serfdom, endlessly commenting on the "authorities," like those clerics who take refuge in repetition, clinging for dear life to what they have, and maintaining vigilant guard to hold on to what has been believed "everywhere, always, and by everyone," to cite Vincent of Lerins (A.D. 434). In 1975, Paul VI also reminded the delegates of SECAM that: "In matters of Christian faith, we must hold to the identical, essential, constitutional patrimony of Christ's own doctrine, as proposed by the authentic and authoritative tradition of the one, true Church."[6]

The tensions and conflicts inherent in the life of our communities deny us any intellectual complacency. In black Africa, the catechisms used for teaching are generally only a condensation of Christian theology that empties God's plan of any historical dimension. We were evangelized in the universe of the Counter-Reformation, with both its greatness and its servility. To truly claim a faith that comes from elsewhere, we must free ourselves from a Christianity that is barren and abstract.

An entire generation of Christians received the gospel in a socio-religious context where every aspect of Christian life was interpreted in moralizing terms. The Christianity of the missions tended to cover up the Good News in favor of the law and its obligations. The Word of God was reduced to commandments, which were preserved by a church whose pyramidal structure restricted the faithful to the demeaning task of receiving orders from on high and passing them on. Sin itself was taught as a moral fault—more precisely, the breaking of a juridical code. We are from an epoch of faith where the celebration of the mystery of salvation itself was reduced to "religious practice," and, as such, fell into the category of obligation. Today it is dangerous to subject Africans to a mixture of these pious fantasies, mingled with the true faith. At a time when all forces are converging to throw the churches of Africa into a crusade against materialism, talk about the Christian faith must be vigilant against foundering in international power plays that are as simplistic as they are Machiavellian.

African Christianities have increased with great vigor. They are now in danger of being used to console a church that has lost its momentum in maturing societies. In order to snatch poor blacks from damnation, missioners need only preach internal conversion. A recent colloquium with a radically pious theme left no room to grasp the challenges in today's Africa—challenges from which the Word of God must be spoken and celebrated. It seemed as if spirituality itself was the only way to salvation for millions of African souls. Yet too much is at stake. We must be vigilant in rethinking our faith and in using all its critical power to serve the gospel in Africa. Overwhelmed by a heavy heritage of obediently parroting dogmatic formulas, we cannot approach any aspect of Christianity without continuing to reevaluate critically the overall structures of the colonial churches.

We do not know what we believe unless we say it in our own language. Until now, the African churches have spoken a kind of Christian "creole" that includes expressions from translations of the catechism going back to Trent. We must re-hear everything previously spoken about God and God's revelation to people in all times, all languages, and all cultures. If everything were fixed for all time, we would be useless to the world of faith. But this is not so. By accepting the mission to announce the gospel to their peoples, the churches of Africa must take up the gospel once again, and rethink it so they can announce the Good News in a new way.

The Risk of an African Interpretation

Revelation is never passively received. The West has never stopped reading or talking about Christianity, but it has always done so based on its fantasies of collective anxiety and hope. What reaches us from the gospel is always a phenomenon within the history of a people, which, in turn, is strongly mediated by socio-cultural factors. It is not simply a question of words or concepts rooted in the history of ideas and beliefs. It is also the awareness a society has of itself, which is translated into the language produced by the church to express its faith. The formulation of doctrines, catechetical texts, treatises of theology, missionary preaching, forms of piety, and church institutions always leads us back to a certain vision of humanity and of the world, to a perception of space and time, and to a style of human relationships. People have always expected to receive the words of the Lord together with the authorized commentary of tradition and church teaching; but, in reality, what they have actually received is the language of a society, with its major questions, its specific needs and most important concerns, a certain sensitivity to the questions of a given time, and a mentality specific to a given people. Since interpretation of the gospel never exhausts the potential of meaning inherent in the message and practice of Jesus Christ, there is always something new to hear and to discover. The basic task of African Christianity is to extract the core of meaning of the gospel through listening to God in the context of our communities.

The church in Rome can no longer think of itself as the sole legitimate repository of the patrimony of Christian faith and doctrine. Perhaps the church needs much more fraternal humility before it can admit that the mysteries of Christianity cannot be proclaimed through repetition of the same words and formulas. The particular experiences of young churches must be expressed in theological currents that have no need for the blessing of schools of theology or their licensed teachers. The church needs only to listen to others for a language of faith to germinate—a language that will be something more than a rehash of existing theologies, touched up for passing needs. If we allow the Lord of the church enough freedom, it is possible that doctrinal truth will be spoken and translated in the whole spectrum of languages and cultures. The universalism of Christianity is not an established fact; it simply appears on the horizon of a promise that comes true in the dialectical tension produced by the confrontation of different cultures.

How can the African become a contemporary of Jesus Christ? We must constantly seek to answer this question in our churches, as other communities have done throughout history. As we try to respond, we, in turn, are only expressing the historical and cultural distance separating us from the gospel. Since the true scandal of faith is the intervention of God in history, we cannot avoid asking ourselves how to talk about God and live our faith in the realm of meaning where Africans try to speak about themselves and the world. We must seriously consider the intercultural dimension of evangelization. The epoch has ended in which the West was the cultural oven baking the intellectual bread of Catholicism. Non-European peoples have arrived on the world scene, and there is now a need to inculturate the faith. If we refuse to base the encounter of the church with Africa on symbolic violence, we must acknowledge that we can no longer believe except by interpreting.

The recitation of formulas is no longer important to us. What is important is that we try to extricate the contemporary meaning of the Word of God and of the plan of salvation, beginning with the historical understanding that Africans have of themselves and of the world. We must exercise this hermeneutical function of theology when we are invited to understand ourselves in the light of revelation, and to perceive the profound meaning of the situations and events which mark our historical destiny. We would rather see the African theologian turn to the Bible than to the dogmatics of the church. Isn't a theologian above all a hearer of the Word? Theologians must let themselves be converted by the Word of God in order to search for other possible paths toward a new understanding of Christ.

The experience of faith is marked by tensions and discords that are born in black Africa from the encounter of the church with ancestral culture. In African villages or slums, a relationship with the invisible is part of the experience of faith of Christians. This obsession or fascination with the occult must not be ignored by the churches. Although it was thought that the practice of sorcery would disappear along with changes in African society, its revival forces us to reconsider all of our talk about faith in terms of the "world of the night," with its well-known hold on Africans. If theology wants to avoid the meaninglessness of purely verbal orthodoxy, which produces generalizations that interest no one, it must take into account what is actually lived in the particular experience of African local communities.

Many African Christians question the invisible forces at work in the universe. Communication between the visible and the invisible opens up a vast field of research. African theologians must question the Christian mystery in terms of a vision of the world where the invisible has genuine reality. No manual of theology contains a programmed response to all the questions that agitate the bush villages, the city slums, and the élites in power who ape a foreign life style while they continue to consult all kinds of merchants of illusion, indigenous healers, and marabouts. The daily life of Christian communities is where African theology should develop. If we wish to maintain a living connection between the communal experience of faith and theological discourse, we must stop dogmatizing in order to consider again all the questions that the first evangelization of Africa left unanswered.

It will not be sufficient to take into account the African experience of the spoken word, which would doubtlessly bring unexpected depth to our approach to God's Word. What must be incorporated, before anything else, is the tragedy of the original break between God and humanity, which is attested to in most of the cultural centers of Africa. How are we to learn all over again to talk about God in a context where the people understand that God ceased to reveal himself, turning humanity over to drought, suffering, and death, as the ancient Zulgo people of northern Cameroon believe. The myths of the African peoples challenge Christian theology and turn the best lessons of our most "qualified" theologians into almost useless baggage. They cannot face the penetrating questions of our old sages who can neither read nor write. Words coming from elsewhere accomplish nothing; they lose their meaning. How many theologians from the well-known schools anticipated the questions being asked today by illiterate peasants? We must be aware of these obstacles if we are to understand the descent of Jesus Christ into hell in terms of the African who is faced with the power of the invisible.

Africans search for happiness in the shadow of their ancestors.

We must join them there if Africans are to surmise the truth in our statements of faith, our preaching of eternal life, and our expectation of another world. Using this point of view, the field of symbolic forces gives us a different view of the signs and means of salvation.

Similarly, the African way of death challenges our reading of the Passion narratives. The theme of redemptive sacrifice has always been examined according to thought patterns defined by the West, which even today dehumanizes death. In our African cultures where the rites that accompany death consolidate the links of kinship, and where the beating of the drums, the dance, and the funeral "palaver" clearly indicate that the accent is on the *positive* side of death, what understanding of redemptive death is required? It seems that our theology of redemption must be reworked and based on a tradition that asks, as a Bantu myth puts it, "What would life be without death?" The importance of these issues can be seen in the broad African context where the relationship of humanity to the universe is integrated into the drama of life and death. We must rethink Christianity itself, taking into account the words and gestures through which people participate in this fundamental drama of life and death.

The answers to these problems will never come from the scholastic tradition of our catechisms; rather, we must translate our relationship with Jesus of Nazareth into the language of our culture. Such an approach requires a sort of "ethics of transgressions," by which we dare to break with the dogmatization of categories of thought, the formulas, and the gestures of faith that carry no characteristics of the African people. We will not move a step ahead in working out an African theology until we agree to run the risk of doing our own interpreting.

Also, if we are going to submit revelation to the new examination demanded by the Vatican Council, we must resolutely face the fundamental conditions of Africans who confront the hostility of nature, of drought and of insecurity. They ask, "How can we escape famine and death? How can we stay in good health, find peace, and put the world back together again?" The African churches should also be concerned with the need for security which obsesses the helpless masses. We need to reread the gospel on the actual scene where people seek reconciliation with the invisible powers, and protection from occult forces. African theology has to consider peoples' circumstances in the world and overcome the conflicts disturbing them; theology must also consider the social context that determines peoples' attitudes toward evil and exist- ence. In short, the whole symbolic structure of the imaginary should challenge our theological reflection.

It will certainly be necessary to come out from our ivory towers to encounter the real Africa, to interpret the "today" of God in the daily life of our people, with an acute awareness of the problems posed by practicing faith in a given culture. We must stay in communion with the people of God—the only adequate subject of theology and faith. And this is already underway in several regions of Africa.

Inculturation of the faith has made it possible to do research to illuminate the choices open to local churches. A number of studies deal with enhancing the use of African symbolism in the Christian mystery. The same is true of the right to live one's Christianity as an African while seriously considering the problems presented to the faith by the veneration of the ancestors. Similarly, establishing a connection between faith and health witnesses to the ministry of healing that plays such a prominent role in the New Testament.

In many places throughout Africa, an approach to the Christian mystery from the viewpoint of what Africans *are* is no longer just a pious wish. In Burkina Faso, an encounter with Bobo initiation has stimulated the pastoral and theological reflections of Anselme Sanon.[7] In Benin, where traditional religions remain dynamic, Adoukounou shows how the debate between Christianity and voo- doo presents guidelines for an African theology.[8] J. Agossou is working along similar lines with the separate realities of the people of Dahomey and their God.[9] In Mali, Bishop Sidbe Semporé is exploring the world of the Bambara from the viewpoint of an encounter with Christ.[10]

Investigations along similar lines are going on in the major African seminaries, in centers for catechetical and pastoral studies, and in houses for religious training. A catalogue of articles and theses by ecclesiastical students in Africa, in Rome, and in other faculties of theology would give an idea of the scope of this movement that sees religious anthropology as the privileged setting for African theology.[11] The desire to reclaim for ourselves a faith that has come from the West has exerted itself equally in Zaire, where the church has been brutally confronted by a policy of authenticity. Various publications, including the *Semaines Théologiques* of the Catholic Faculty of Theology at Kinshasa, show that our need to find a better expression of the faith—one corresponding to African realities—can lead to a methodological approach that takes into account our socio-cultural context. Aylward Shorter maintains that African theology must be the fruit of a dialogue between the living African tradition and Christianity.[12]

Inculturation Set Adrift

Within the diversity of the Third World, everything still happens as if black churches can achieve their identity by considering only anthropological and cultural problems. One cannot really disguise the ambiguity of such efforts at theological research that are positioned first of all in the realm of traditional culture. There is a certain risk in doing the work of an antiquarian while "things fall apart," in the words of Chinua Achebe.

We are living through the difficulties of a transitional epoch where African identity is itself not fully defined. The invasion of the life of Africans by a foreign world disrupts every aspect of their universe. Independent churches, sects, the phenomena of possession, and the revival of sorcery are all features of the present crisis affecting African culture and society. The temptation to "recapture" tradition can be a dangerous alibi, even though no theology can exist cut off from the history of human beings and the movements that affect them. Today's tragedies, internal lacerations, and challenges are the place where a culture is being born out of a people's struggle to rediscover its memory and regain its dignity. We have to build connections between Christian theology and an African culture that is marked by the socio-historical dynamism of contemporary Africa. The theological effort needed by the African churches cannot be limited to the cult of the past.

Today Africa is subject to conditionings far more effective than the values of tradition. Urbanization, contemporary economic constraints, the phenomenal increase in school enrollment, the growth of unemployment, drought, and famine are phenomena completely upsetting human conditions in black Africa. The tasks of our faith require that Christianity confront the structures and mentalities emerging from the collision between the black world and other peoples. The claim that Africa is "incurably religious" must be demystified. Our societies are no longer sheltered against secularization, atheism, or religious indifference. We need only read African literature to realize the attitude of the new generations toward Christian missions. The disaffection of a large part of the intelligentsia is a serious challenge to the African church. Faced with the invasion of sects into university campuses and intellectual circles, we can no longer entertain comfortable illusions of security. Why should we orient theological research around rites and beliefs alone, while modernity causes the masses to be aware of another set of problems?

Instead of talking complacently about inculturation, which, in the end, never stops singing the praises of *négritude* and authenticity, we should prepare ourselves to confront the basic questions of the Africa that is evolving today. African culture is what we live; it cannot be reduced to music and dance. Any appraisal of the problems of faith organized narrowly around the recovery of the past will never allow us to stand beside Africans as they ask their questions of today. In Kampala, Paul VI applauded *négritude*, just when in Algiers, it was being dismissed as obsolete.

African churches must resist the temptation to link theological reflection to that "authenticity" that appears today as an ideology masking the stalemate of the ruling classes that are prey to the increasing difficulties of underdevelopment. Instead of recasting the economy to serve the most defenseless, the élites in power have generated a discourse intended to cover up their failure. The return to "authenticity" satisfies the illusions of a middle class cut off from the people, and diverts the masses from their true problems. African culture is being manipulated by repressive régimes whose objective is to keep the mass of the people in misery and dependence. Those who have received privileges from the régimes in power do not hesitate, from time to time, to restore certain customs and traditions, usually traditions that have been emptied of their content. Yet they continue to play games with the economic forces pillaging Africa today. After years of questioning and groping, we have reached a turning point; self-evaluation and revision are now essential.

Our theologians had to inquire if it was possible, in the name of faith, to be a Christian without denying that one was also an African. The question could not be sidestepped since Africa was a land where humanity had been treated with contempt for centuries and where Africans had been denied their cultural identity for too long. The deep aspirations of generations who professed *négritude* restored dignity and affirmed an African presence in the world. This turn of events led to the publication in 1956 of the book *Des prêtres noirs s'intérrogent* (*Some Black Priests Question Themselves*).[13] Some people have not yet extricated themselves from the type of problems taken up in this manifesto; they continue today to reproduce and repeat the same questions. We have not yet gone beyond the point of challenging the thesis of Lévy-Bruhl concerning the "prelogical mentality" of primitive peoples. Some observers have naturally concluded that nothing new has been produced in Africa since *Des prêtres noirs s'intérrogent*.

What is especially troubling is not the monotony of this discourse, but its theological weakness. For twenty years, the bulk of studies and publications have focused on indigenization or Africanization in a reaction to cultural imperialism at work within the churches. The necessity to respect African cultural identity has been constantly reaffirmed, referring to Acts 15:28, as have the relevant decrees and recommendations of the Congregation for the Evangelization of Peoples—though seldom practiced by missionary institutes. Today there is an obligation to change the appearance of the church and this requires greater creativity. This line of research was actually encouraged by Paul VI during his trip to Africa in 1969 and again by John Paul II in his statements on Africanization in 1980.

After a period of rejection and disdain of indigenous cultures, African studies in the church have concentrated on seeking out the characteristic elements and symbols of a given culture, with an eye to their "adaptation" in catechesis, liturgy, and pastoral work. This anthropological approach has been primary, and has accented differences. Most studies have taken the form of anthropological monographs proposing that the church begin to appropriate cultural data. This base of reflection presupposes an understanding of African religions in which there is an effort to discover in Christ the truth of traditional beliefs and rites. This line of research seemed mandatory since evangelization was continuing in a society based on African culture and religions. "Theology" appeared in the wake of ethnology, with its tendency to camouflage the actual contradictions of African society and its need to struggle to escape from the neo-colonial yoke. This preoccupation with what is "typically African" runs the danger of ignoring the historical factors that condition the production of theological knowledge itself.

Within this "indigenist" framework that has dominated research for twenty years, questions raised about the destiny of the African personality within Catholicism have not affected the Church's attitude toward power in Africa, where political and military *coups d'états* dominate daily life. It hasn't really mattered as the church has given way before the forces of repression, enclosed in a silence of complicity when confronted with authorities who oppress and extort a people and yet try to appropriate their lifestyle, art, mentality, rites, and proverbs. Life has continued as if the concentration of power in the hands of an individual or group, and the rise of bloody dictatorships that control the people do not create new conditions affirming a vision of humanity and of the world, often in opposition to the traditional systems, which administered collective life and mediated conflict through "palaver."

But how is it possible to study the people's culture without becoming uneasy about the marginalization of those masses whose folkways have become the object of anthropological research? This question is important because the movement, which has been called indigenization, Africanization, or inculturation of the faith, has occurred at the same time as the formation of the African states. At a time when a single political party serves as a screen on which Africans are superimposed to legitimate foreign domination, we cannot be satisfied with reflection on faith and culture that is limited to the study of beliefs and rites.

Christian communities starting to live out their faith at the grassroots have been preoccupied with the concentration of wealth in the hands of a minority, the corruption suffered by the poor in the villages and shanty-towns, the dispossession of peasants and small herdsmen, and even torture. The tragedy of the kind of theological discourse that has prevailed up to now is that it totally ignores these Christian communities, although they are rooted in the soil and confront new challenges. Perhaps certain changes will come about when African Christians are "conscientized." Perhaps we need to realize that it is the Christian community here and now that should conscientize theologians and pastors.

In any case, we have said enough about the relationship between faith and culture. This discussion was indeed essential for working out an African theology, to point out that the West itself has awakened to recognize these differences. But now we must move beyond this discussion if we are to reflect on the meaning of our faith as Africans.

A Theology Coming from the People

What kind of theology will truly respond to African hopes? The African bishops have recently proposed moving from a "theology of adaptation" to a "theology of incarnation"; but, upon closer inspection, the latter is still oriented around the problems of Africanization. Since culture cannot be treated in isolation from the problems of society as a whole, the exploitation that victimizes most Africans obliges us to redefine the fundamental project of Christianity in Africa. At a time when many people expect the church to act as the conscience of society, we need to examine more seriously this "incarnation of Christianity" from the perspective of the forgotten ones of the earth.

Africa is turning into a continent for others, catapulted into the ambiguous adventure of modernity where the "suns of independence" simply do not shine on the masses crammed into native quarters. A reading of African reality that treats the cultural data of our societies only as stepping stones or as a "preparation for the gospel" will pass over in silence any effort to reinterpret African culture on the basis of the challenges of history, or of its need for survival, defense, or resistance.

Myths about Africa have served as a framework for understanding the colonial situation, creating a world that is both unique and universal, and that justifies and explains the inequities between whites and blacks. Awareness of the conditions of poverty of the blacks was occasionally expressed in the theme of the curse, which incorporates characteristics of the colonial ideology and aspects of the traditional African world. A legend of the Fang people traces the poverty of the blacks and the wealth of the whites back to a divine decree![14] In Benin and Togo, Adoukounou reports a myth of the superiority of whites and the inferiority of blacks. As he recalls, it consists of a reworking of the motif from traditional mythology of the elder and younger son, placed in the context of the brutal encounter between Africa and the West.[15] It would be useful to reexamine these stories, proverbs, legends, myths, collective beliefs, songs, and the language of the drums to rediscover the forms of black protest against colonial domination. An historical event of this magnitude cannot have left the popular imagination wholly indifferent and passive. We need to go back to actual history, and locate the most profound symbols of African culture in a broader context, a context that bears the marks of domination and conflict. The stories that Africa tells about its life and its past are of great interest for our understanding of the Christian faith. A whole world emerges through them, a world that we must attentively grasp and understand, and a world from which we must learn all we can.

At a time when millions of black peasants are working—not to feed themelves but to sell for a wholly inadequate price export crops that will bring in foreign exchange and profit only an urban minority—African theologians must listen to their people who ask themselves, "How long will this go on, my God?" There is a need to break loose from the dominant theology that has monopolized the church's attention far too long with its internal problems. The question of "God" is being asked today from the bottom of society, there where racism and segregation develop and where famine results from a policy of domination rather than from natural disasters due to climate.

The problem of African theology, then, is not so much located on the level of discourse as on the level of concrete commitment as men and women apply themselves to those tasks that show the commitment of the church to stand by those mired down by history. The countries of Africa are seeking to emerge from poverty by means of programs of assistance that will unquestionably only further enslave them. In contrast, the church must promote a Christianity that will help the African masses get out of the deadlock that has followed independence, and a Christianity that will become a force resisting injustice and exploitation. The theology being sought is one committed to respond to the "cry of the African." As the Accra meeting suggested:

> African theology must reject, therefore, the prefabricated ideas of North Atlantic theology by defining itself according to the struggles of the people in their resistance against the structures of domination. Our task as theologians is to create a theology that arises from and is accountable to the African people.[16]

What are the chances of this happening in the churches of Africa, where too often the most striking phenomenon is the silence maintained by churches and missioners alike with respect to the dictatorship of the single-party politics, to repression, and to the growing control of multinational corporations—which are far from being benevolent associations? The expression of a certain number of ideas in the domain of theology is tolerated, provided that they remain inaccessible to Christian communities, which, in contrast, are subjected to a system of control that benefits the established disorder. But, in fact, to what extent have the churches of Africa officially adopted the positions of the African theologians who put together the manifesto of Dar es Salaam (1976)? What impact was made on them by the declaration of the Pan-African Assembly of Accra in 1977, which explicitly stated that African theology must develop from a "commitment to the struggles of our people for their liberation"?

It is possible today that ecclesial authorities can use the discourse of African theologians without in any way modifying their actual practices. Then even a theology that comes from the people becomes the business of a very small group, and it can still be used as a kind of alibi. The danger of such a theology is that it could be adopted by those people who occupy positions of power at the heart of the African churches. In black Africa, the vast majority of the religious authorities are chosen, admitted or tolerated only on the condition that they keep silent on the essential problems of daily life. Contradictions exist even inside the churches. How can a theology arise out of these structures that have been eternally imposed on our people, in a dominated society where the voice of the gospel is stifled in order to guarantee the stability of unpopular régimes or the prosperity of foreign investments? It is not all that easy to do theology in countries where the churches almost seem to be pillars of the neo-colonial state.

Today we can observe a sort of counteroffensive against the currents of liberation that have caught up the younger generations, with the goal of imprisoning African Christians in the formulas of Roman theology. It would be a tragedy for African theologians to isolate themselves in a situation controlled by a uniform language that can mask the contradictions and conflicts of African society during the changes of today. But we have to run this risk. The African churches are waiting for loud voices that will announce the gospel with boldness, and courageously denounce torture, exploitation, and the oppression of the majority by a minority who often serve only foreign interests.

Notes

1. See the bibliography on "African Theology" drawn up by R. Facélina & D. Rwzgera, *Théologie africaine* (Strasbourg: RTC, 1977).

2. "Ad Gentes," 22 in *Vatican Council II: The Conciliar and Post Conciliar Documents*, edited by Austin Flannery (Northport, NY: Costello, 1975), pp. 22-23.

3. See the *Déclaration sur l'évangélisation dans la corresponsabilité* (D. 1664), 1974.

4. See the studies gathered in *Civilisation noire et Église catholique* (Paris: Présence Africaine, 1977).

5. Sidbe Semporé, "The Churches in Africa between Past and Future," *Concilium* 106 (1977), p. 7.

6. "Faith: Source and Goal of Evangelization," Address of Pope Paul VI to SECAM (September 26, 1975) in *The Pope Speaks* 20 (1975): 269-270.

7. Anselme Sanon, *Tièrce Église, ma mère: ou, la conversion d'une communauté païenne au Christ* (Paris: Beauchesne, 1972).

8. B. Adoukounou, *Jalons pour une théologie africaine. Essai d'une herméneutique chrétienne du Vaudou dahoméen* (Paris: Lethielleux, 1980), 2 vols.

9. J.-B. Agossou, *Gbeto et Gbedoto: l'homme et le Dieu créateur selon les Sud-Dahoméens. De la dialectique de la participation vitale à une théologie anthropocentrique* (Paris: Beauchesne, 1972).

10. Sidbe Semporé, *La rencontre de Jésus-Christ en milieu bambara* (Paris: Beauchesne, 1978).

11. M. Meslin, "Vers une théologie africaine," *Les Quatres Fleuves* 10 (1979), pp. 117-131.

12. A. Shorter, *African Christian Theology: Adaptation or Incarnation?* (London: Chapman, 1975).

13. *Des prêtres noirs s'interrogent* (Paris: Présence Africaine, 1956; 2nd ed., Paris: Cerf, 1957).

14. R. Bureau, *La religion d'Eboga,* vol. 1, pp. 196-197.

15. B. Adoukounou, *Jalons pour une théologie africaine. Essai d'une herméneutique chrétienne du Vaudou dahoméen* (Paris: Lethielleux, 1980), pp. 8-10.

16. "Final Communiqué, Pan African Conference of Third World Theologians, December 17-23, 1977, Accra, Ghana," in *African Theology En Route,* edited by Appiah-Kubi and Torres (Maryknoll, NY: Orbis, 1979), p. 193.

Conclusion

Theology under the Tree

Faith, which is the way God wants me to look at my situation in the world, leads me to discover that the reality of paganism is the death and slavery to which black peoples are condemned. Faith is also the proclamation of a God who saves humanity from this paganism. In my opinion, the crisis of meaning at the heart of our time lies within this faith. The reponsibility to live our faith and speak of God therefore becomes enormous, for it puts the world on trial at the same time as it overthrows idols, including the idol of a God who is not committed to the victory of humanity. The whole problem of culture and faith and its language is rooted in this profound experience.

I have to recognize that this small book will not end the debate going on today wherever Africa and the gospel confront one another. But it is very clear to me that it is becoming more and more dangerous to speak about God if nothing concrete can verify the statements that conform to Christian dogma. We glimpse the dangers of blasphemy and of betrayal to which churches open themselves when human distress and situations of death provide more evidence each day for the trial of the God whom they announce. The plan of God the Creator and Savior is endangered and blocked by the failure of our systems and the deadlock brought about by structures that unceasingly burden us.

Today, considering all of this, what story can we tell about God as we recall Jesus Christ? Evidently we must return to the tree of the cross to remake theology, starting with the struggles of black people

179

to prevent their world from being plunged back into the chaos that reigned before creation. In that sense, doing theology is no longer an academic exercise, but a spiritual adventure. That is why what is happening today in the villages and slums of Africa prevents theologians from shutting their eyes and drifting off to sleep with the purring of a clear conscience—created by producing the type of discourse that, up until now, has been oriented around demands for indigenization and acculturation.

It is revealing that Africanization and authenticity is usually the only language tolerated within African churches. It is the same language spoken by the authorities in countries where the people not only suffer the effects of cultural imperialism, but also find themselves politically and economically excluded from decision-making and from any sharing of the national resources. Today mass media, schools, and the ideology of development all reinforce domination in black Africa, in concert with the rest of the ideological apparatus. Yet the explosive force of people and groups in villages and shanty-towns, working to get themselves out of dependency and injustice, is the place where a theology will emerge that renounces talk about God and faith on the basis of a ready-made "revelation." If God speaks through history, theology can no longer be learned through the words of manuals that simply perpetuate from one generation to another a faith that has been defined once and for all. Theology in our time can be learned only in the act of liberating the poor.

I dream of a "theology under the tree," which would be worked out as brothers and sisters sit side by side wherever Christians share the lot of peasant people who seek to take responsibility for their own future and for transforming their living conditions. In order for that to happen, people must leave the libraries and give up the comfort of air-conditioned offices; they must accept the conditions of life in the insecurity of study in poor areas where the people have their feet in water or in mud and can neither read nor write.

Perhaps this theology will not use the vocabulary of scholars and philosophers. But didn't God also speak the language of peasants and shepherds in order to be revealed to humanity? We must rediscover the oral dimension of theology, which is no less important than the *summae* and the great treatises. Christian theology must be liberated from a cultural system that sometimes conveys the false impression that the Word has been made text. Why can't the language of faith also be poetry, song, game, art, dance, and above all the gesture of humanity standing up and marching wherever the gospel elicits and nourishes a liberating effort? To create a poetics of faith, we must rediscover the African soul, or *anima*, where symbol appeals through metaphor and helps us speak of that God who raises up the meek and feeds the hungry.

Such a step cannot come about in isolation. A theology in context must also be a theology in dialogue, open to exchange and confrontation. African theology requires a deepening of the methods involved in working out any theology; it also needs to let itself be questioned by all the theologies based on the solidarity of peoples, continents, or groups struggling for the coming of a new world. Certainly that will not happen without free and responsible theological work.

When Cardinal Ratzinger, secretary of the Congregation for the Doctrine of the Faith, states that he "harbors some anxiety" about the Ecumenical Association of African Theologians, the question must be raised whether he is speaking and reacting as a theologian or as a functionary of the church. In either case, for him to say that African theologians risk neglecting the value of the great Catholic unity in favor of "more restricted cultural communities" implies that this unity can be safeguarded only in the structures of churches that are still under tutelage. But if all theologies no longer come from Rome, Rome must open its ears to hear what is being said about God in the local churches.

Instead of imposing silence on the theologians of the Third World, the church in Rome must show itself able to live within the conflict of differing hermeneutics, without letting either distrust or fear govern its control in the service of the faith. Disciplinary procedures could paralyze the theological reflection that is striving now to establish the coherence of dogmas within the context of African culture and society. Indispensable, above all, in Africa is a climate that will allow us to design a style for living our faith in the midst of our current contradictions and hidden dependencies. Meinrad Hebga has asked:

> Will we have the courage, the audacity, the temerity, even the possibility to start again from zero and draw an intelligible

discourse from the sources of Revelation, a discourse that is accessible to our people? Let's not secretly work to agree with our masters and be approved by them so that they can find our discourse reducible in one way or another to their own system?[1]

And if we are to do that, we must end the proxy held until now by Western churches in the realm of theology. We must give each local church responsibility for its own theological thinking. We must bring about the decentralization of producing "official" theological meaning, and we must end the seclusion of theological discourse in the West.

One thing is certain. Christian theology has entered a new era. The task at hand is to pass from a conflict of cultures to a culture of confrontation. At a time when the unbridled expansion of the affluent is constantly tightening the noose that strangles Africa, we must return to our people, become their companions in life and their travelling partners. Even though it may be suicidal, that is the only possible outcome for theologians who no longer want to live as spectators or hermits.

Hence, the great challenge to faith and to theology in Africa is our historical situation that snatches Christianity out of meaninglessness, and restores its relevance in the places of tension where the midwives of the future and the witnesses of freedom are to be found. We live in a continent marked by supposedly inescapable unhappiness, a continent where poverty alone seems to have a prosperous future. Where are the men and women who have made up their minds to sow life, so that hope may germinate? How can the Easter message once again become a well where Christians and churches can draw strength to march ahead? "O Death, where is thy victory?" That is the question I ask myself, in my faith as an African, as the third millennium draws near.

Note

1. M. Hebga, *Émancipation d'églises sous tutelle* (Paris: Présence Africaine, 1976), p. 83.

Index

Achebe, C., 170
Adoukounou, B., 169, 175
Africanization: as focus of theological research, 172–173; language of, 147; and *négritude,* 145; pitfalls of, 145–148; as task of Africans, 145; and theological reflection, 162
Agossou, J., 169
agriculture: and ancestral religion, 8; domination of, by export crops, 69, 71; modernization of, 70, 88–89, 150; in northern Cameroon, 4
ancestor cult, 8, 119, 166–168, 169; abandonment of, 25–26; ancestor as mediator, 22; and art, 15; and Christian faith, 13–31; responsibility of descendants to, 16; role of sacrifice and diviner in, 21–24; *see also* kinship system
arms race, 117
atheism, 87–88, 100
authenticity, 171
Baba Simon, 3, 94
Bachelard, 42
Bakole wa Ilunga, 131
baptism, 48, 50, 57–58, 140, 144, 155
Beti, M., 140
Bishops Conference of Cameroon, 137

blackness. *See négritude*
canon law, 144
capitalism: and exploitation of peasant agriculture, 88–90, 152; and expression of Christianity, 149; and health care, 69–70; resistance to, 97–98; and rural development, 150–151
Casaroli, Cardinal, 127
catechesis, 8, 10, 11, 110
celibacy, 58
China, 13, 20
Christianity: changing mission in Third World, 91; imported practices, 122–123; indigenization of, 121–122; innovations in, 115; need for credibility, 119, 130–135; need to reexamine centralized structure, 116, 120; obsolescence of, 122; subversive nature of, 109–110, 128, 133
Christianity, African: challenges facing, 154, 170–171, 182; converts, 138; established through mission experience, 10–11; and mass media, 160; present condition of, 33–34; role of, 165, 174; *see also* churches, local
church: as free space for study, 138
church, Roman, 99, 154, 165
churches, local, 34, 129–130, 131, 143; choices available to, 169;

183

see also Christianity, African; communities, Christian

circumcision. *See* initiation

class structure: and health care, 69, 70–74

cleanness and uncleanness, 106–107, 109

clergy: celibacy, 58; indigenous, 121–122, 127; lack of, 58–59, 62, 146, 163; preoccupation of, with ritual, 140, 149; search of, for rural model, 121–122; silence of, 137, 176; tyranny of, 55–60

colonialism, 118, 125, 155; and Christianity, 111; and health care, 67–69; and myths about Africa, 174

colors: symbolism, 48

communication, traditional, 10, 44–47

communities, Christian, 91–92, 94–95; autonomy of, 163; ignored in theological research, 173–174; leadership within, 60–64; need for, 146; and Old Testament, 127–128

community: liturgical celebration of, 7–8, 26–27; president, 61; as sacrament, 6–12

confession, 61, 140

confirmation, 57–58, 155

Congregation for the Doctrine of the Faith, 181

Congregation for the Evangelization of Peoples, 172

Cosmao, V., 95

cotton, 4; *see also* millet

credibility: Christianity's need for, 119, 130–135

crucifixion, 108–112, 128

culture, African: Christianity

rooted in, 119, 120–121; evolution in history, 148–151

death, 20–21, 41, 168

decolonization, 116, 118, 156

Deniel, R., 24

descendants: responsibility toward ancestors, 16

DeSouza, I., 145

development, 150; community based, 97–98; new model of, 100; and peasant society, 88–89

diaconate, 56, 59–60

diviner, 21–24, 51, 140

Dumont, R., 89

Easter, 6, 110, 182; *see also* resurrection

East-West conflict, 117

Eboussi Boulaga, F., 139

Ecumenical Association of African Theologians, 181

education, 9, 122, 124, 151, 153

evangelization: and "human promotion," 130–131; and traditional oral culture, 44–47

exploitation. *See* oppression

export crops, 147, 150, 175; *see also* capitalism; food crops

famine: profits from, 118

Fanon, F., 148

Feast of All Saints, 29, 30

Feast of All Souls, 30

Festival of the Bull. *See Maray*

food crops: displaced by cash crops, 4, 92, 96–97; *see also* millet

foods, symbolism of, 35–36, 38, 48–50

foreign investment, 96, 118

funerals, 61

funerary jar. *See pra*

gospel: African reading of, 102–105, 142; call to refute oppression, 126–130; consequences of living, 132–134; identification with the miserable, 156; and justification of oppression, 111; as liberation, 155; subordination to interests of the powerful, 105; subversive power of, 152

granary, 37, 92–99; as image of the world, 45; and *pra,* 15

healing. *See* sickness

healing, Christian, 141, 169

health care: and colonialism, 67–69; cost of, 124; and missions, 75–76, 82, 84–85, 151; and social systems, 69–75, 81, 83; *see also* sickness

Hegba, M., 181

Hegel, G. W., 139

history, interpretation of one's own, 115

housing and hygiene, 71, 72

Hugon, P., 71

humanity, break with God, 45, 48, 167

inculturation: 127, 169, 170–174; *see also* Africanization

independence: 89–90, 147, 155, 156, 173, 175; *see also* decolonization

indigenization. *See* inculturation

initiation, traditional, 10, 14, 36, 40–41, 169

invisible world, 16, 21, 141–142; *see also* ancestor cult

irruption of the poor, 90–92, 116, 131

John Paul II, 124, 145, 149, 162, 172

Kabanga Songasonga, 128, 131

Kane, C. H., 12, 101

kinship: and abandonment of tra-ditional practices, 25–26; bonds between generations, 18–20; and death, 168; as symbol of world view, 17; *see also* ancestor cult

Kirdi, 5, 12

laity, 56–64

language: indigenous Christian, 5, 29–31, 164; linguistic imperialism, 165; of the spirit, 144–145; *see also* communication, traditional; literacy; naming

Lazarus, 106, 127

Linhart, R., 96

literacy: 9, 46, 93; *see also* education

liturgy: local rites, 13–14; pluralism in young churches, 26; use of African elements in, 27, 46–47, 144, 147

magic, 140

Manes (spirits of ancestors), 18

marabouts. *See* diviners

Maray (Festival of the Bull), 17, 24

mass media, 157, 160

Mbiti, J., 19

meal: use as symbol, 48–50

mediator, 22–23

messianism: and oppression, 102–105

Metz, J., 128

millet: displaced by cotton, 4, 100, 150; God's command to grow, 5, 88; *see also* granary

ministry: of the granary, 92–99; theology of, 55–60

missions: as agent of liberation, 99; failure to enter into African life, 90; and health care, 75–76, 82, 84–85

Moingt, J., 60

multinational corporations, 128,

176; *see also* capitalism

Mveng, E., 40

Myre, A., 105

naming, 37, 45, 48

négritude, 145, 147, 148, 171, 172

neocolonialism, 126, 147, 152, 153, 155, 156, 157

newborns, ceremony for, 18

Niger, P., 147

Nolan, A., 122–123

non-aligned nations, 116

North-South conflict, 117, 119

nutrition: 69–70, 84; *see also* health care

Nyerere, J., 75, 89, 100, 133, 150

Old Testament: and modern Christian communities, 127–128

oppression: beneficiaries of, 124; and credibility of Christianity, 130–135, 152–153, 175–176; and famine, 147; forms of, 125; gospel call to refute, 105–112, 126–130; as insult to Creator, 152–153; and messianism, 102–105; possibility of change, 111; role of Christianity in, 102, 111, 151–152; *see also* wealth

oppression of peasants to support cities, 150

original sin. *See* humanity, break with God

ouzom i Jegla (Beer of God), 5, 22

pagan. *See* Kirdi

Pan-African Assembly, 176

Pan-African Conference of Third-World Theologians, 125–126

Paul VI: Africanization of Christianity, 26, 115–116, 145, 172; celibacy of priests, 58; liberation of the poor, 153, 155; Message to Africa (1967), 21; *négritude,* 172; neocolonialism,

126; patrimony of Roman church, 163

possession, 51–52, 170

pra: 15, 18, 25;, *see also* ancestor cult

privilege: disturbed by realistic analysis, 118–119

Ratzinger, Cardinal, 181

recolonization, 149

religion: resistance to, 111–112

resurrection, 8, 108–112, 128, 134

revelation, 101, 110, 142, 165

Ricci, M., 13

rice, 150

Sacred Congregation for the Propagation of the Faith, 20

sacrifice, redemptive, 168

saints: and ancestors, 28–29

Sanon, A., 20, 138, 144, 169

scholasticism, 41–44, 163, 168

sects, proliferation of, 34, 119, 120, 140, 154, 170

Sempré, S., 169

Shorter, A., 170

sickness: African view, 21–22, 50–52; as effect of social systems, 81–82; and sin, 77–81

sin: and sickness, 77–81

sorcery: 11, 166, 170; *see also* magic

St. Justin the Apologist, 29

St. Paul, 141, 145

Suffering Servant, 130

symbolism, 6, 48, 141–142; in Christian liturgy, 169; in discourse, 45; importance in Africa, 34–44, 175, 181; kinship and ancestors, 14–18; of meal, 48–50; *see also* ancestor cult

Symposium of Episcopal Conferences of Africa and Madagascar (SECAM), 124, 126, 163